THE TASTE
OF
AIR

THE TASTE
OF
AIR

LAM: A Love Story

RICHARD SCHAD

iUniverse, Inc.
Bloomington

THE TASTE OF AIR
LAM: A LOVE STORY

iUniverse books may be ordered through booksellers or by contacting:

iUniverse
1663 Liberty Drive
Bloomington, IN 47403
www.iuniverse.com
1-800-Authors (1-800-288-4677)

ISBN: 978-1-4759-6023-5 (sc)
ISBN: 978-1-4759-6024-2 (ebk)

Library of Congress Control Number: 2012921586

Printed in the United States of America

iUniverse rev. date: 11/26/2012

All author proceeds from the sale of The Taste of Air go to the LAM Foundation
For further information on LAM or to make a donation, contact
www.thelamfoundation.org

For Karyn, my bashert

PREFACE

I fought with my demons to relive the painful parts of my wife's chronic and potentially life-threatening lung disease. There are so many memories, some ugly, some sweet, and so many bittersweet and all subject to some secret whim when they surface. The past is always your past, yours, even when you try to forget it, the past remembers you. So I take pen to paper to honor the memories, and hope to let them go. It's all I can do.

My hope is that the family of a transplant donor will read this book and find it in their heart of hearts to contact the recipient of their loved one's gift of life, to feel the breathing of their loved one's lungs.

I wish is that a wife suffering from LAM or another suffering from lung disease or cancer will give this book to her husband. She will say, "Honey I think you need to read this book." He will take the book and read it, and after reading the Taste of Air will tell her that the book helped him and he discovered much about himself. I know I did.

Every husband should write the story of his wife. From writing, I appreciate so much more about my wife, and my respect and love have increased tenfold. My wife suffered nearly a total eclipse of her air, but she is here and I am here, and today is much to celebrate. Today, my wife's arms wrap around me like a promise, and that despite everything, all will be well.

May this book in some ways be like when I was little and my mom would rub my back in slow strong circles, and say it would all be okay.

The journey of a chronic disease can be a very dark place, and both caregiver and patient need a candle sometimes. I hope you find yours.

To all who suffer, peace.

Acknowledgments

To Saul Skolnick and Alice Rydeen, both of blessed memory, teachers at Lynwood High School who turned on the switch

To Sue Byrnes, and Fran Byrnes, he of Blessed Memory, founders of the LAM Foundation, who provided the searchlight at the beginning of the Tunnel, cutting through the fog of LAM

To all the surgeons and doctors and nurses and staff at DUKE Medical Center and the DUKE Center for Living. In the beginning there was darkness and you separated the dark from the light and brought unto us the Lamp of Life

To Charlie Levi, who lighted my load, and corrected my multiple errors of tenses, commas, and pronouns. Any errors remaining are the author's own

To Jake, my special Delta Pet Partner therapy dog, of Blessed Memory, whose warm glow brought forth the light of the Sun to all he graced

To our Donor, of Blessed Memory, who brought forth light unto all the nations of our souls. We shall meet when our lives are complete.

THE DAY MY WORLD DIVIDED
BOTH SIDES

I am sitting in the ICU but I cannot see you. Sitting in the waiting room, I straighten my back, and thrust out my chest. I am the bold knight just returned from the Crusades to rescue his fair maiden in 'oft yonder ICU.

A nurse came through the gates of the Castle Keep, the closed double doors of the Intensive Care lung unit at Duke Medical Center, and jubilantly told my sister, Pam, and me, that my wife, Karyn, would be removed from her ventilator shortly, and that she would be back to get both of us in 15 minutes. The nurse would lead us oft to Camelot, to rescue my fair maiden from the tower.

Could it only have been less than two days ago, that my wife received the miracle of life, a double lung transplant from a perfect stranger? What could be more perfect than a person giving you your second chance at life? Like a newborn baby, my wife had received the breath of life, and was newly born.

Fifteen minutes. A moment in time, one of those moments, like JFK or 9/11, I will always remember where I was.

And I am glad I am here. Yesterday I was home in Colorado, taking my first break as primary caregiver, taking care of the house and work. Last night, Karyn was called to the hospital as the primary recipient. I gathered our family at home as we all waited and waited and waited. After twelve hours, my sister Pam, my back-up caregiver, called and said the lungs were "no-good," a "dry-run" and they were going back to the Residence Inn for some much-needed sleep. Early in the morning, before the sun could yawn, the phone rang, and Karyn said she was being called back again to

1

the hospital, but this time Karyn was the secondary back-up. "Don't call the family, I am just the back-up so it probably won't happen." At around 9:00 AM Colorado time, my cell-phone rang, and I answered it, saying, "You and Pam are going back to the hotel to lounge around the pool?" "No, a-jumping-out-of-the-phone, Karyn giggled, "They're wheeling me into surgery right now, it's a go." I could feel her smile in my heart.

I ran around chasing my tail, shaved, showered, packed, and within two hours, I was on a Delta plane heading back to the Promised Land.

The miracle of Karyn, breathing on her own, on room air. Karyn, my wife of 37 years, the love of my life, enjoying her new lungs. Has it been 9 years on supplemental oxygen? Three years waiting for a transplant? I can wait fifteen minutes.

Karyn had been through a nine-hour cakewalk surgery. I almost made it to North Carolina before she was out of surgery. A cakewalk? More like getting run over by a freight train. Make that two freight trains. The nurse had said, "No complications, all signs good." What must it feel like to take a breath, to really breathe, and feel the warmth of your own breath? No tubes in the nose. No cords to get tangled in. No more tanks to fill, and lug around. No more dry nose. I could not wait. God, hurry up those 15 minutes. Your crusader has been waiting for this day for so many years.

I looked over at the wall separating the waiting room from the cubicles of ICU, and imagined I could see through the walls like a super hero, see Karyn on the other side of the wall, and then through her, through her skin, her new lungs, and into my heart. God, I love her more than oxygen. ICU when I breathe. ICU wherever I go. I want to see you. Fifteen minutes.

I slouch back in my seat, and closed my eyes to linger better in my memories and I am instantly transported to that first time I laid my eyes on Karyn. I am amazed that sometimes my vision gets better when I close my eyes. I remember Karyn from that very first moment at a summer camp, some forty-four years ago. You were with one of my friends and he introduced you to me. I do not remember any other part of that camp or any other person's face other than yours. I can't picture my friend, can't see any other place or person at that encampment, but I can see you clearly sitting on that paint-chipped wooden bench.

Reconstructing Karyn's face on the canvas of my mind takes absolutely no effort. I see your tanned face, your browned legs, your white-pink neon lip gloss glistening on your lips, and even your pimply face. I look into your brown eyes, and was charmed instantly by your smile, and I am captured at that moment. I am smitten and I feel a little star struck.

But you were with my friend, which meant you were off-limits, still I remember that scene as if it had happened yesterday. I conjured up another early memory and am transported months later and am at a youth group dance, and I watch this girl dance after dance after dance, as I stand off to the side. I am again mesmerized.

The pull of Karyn Schwartz dancing is almost gravitational. I cannot move from this one spot the entire evening. I stare at her longer than an art history major might look lovingly at the Mona Lisa. There's something beyond beauty in her face, something warm and smart and sensual and inviting and in the six seconds I look at her I actually fall in love, and in those moments, I can actually taste her kiss, the feel of her skin against mine, the sound of her laugh, and how she will look at me and make me whole. I remembered I wasn't flighty or giddy, but grounded as if I had arrived home after a very long travel. As the dance ends, I am standing outside the steps of the dance hall with my friends, and as you leave you turn to us and ask, "Do you know Eric?" We said yes—how do you know him? With that amazing magnetic smile, you tell us to come to your dance the following week, and I am drawn, and I did and we do.

I know I have met someone I will know for the rest of my life. The door to my heart had opened. Sigh. I C U. I still see that little girl with lips of white pink gloss. The pimples are long gone. I knew then, that I have a heart so I can give it to you alone. There really was no getting around her beauty. It was like a warm liquid spreading through my insides, and my perception is nine tenths of the law. I chuckled to myself as I know you do not consider yourself beautiful, but to me you not being perfect is my perfect. God, it is so true that big sweet memories come from such little moments.

They say you never love anyone like the way you love your high school sweetheart. Maybe when an emotion is new, it's like I'm testing it, checking it, to see what the boundaries of it are, and later I feel it even more, even better, even stronger. Maybe not as fresh now but it is ever bit as intense.

At the dance, we shared the same air. The taste is fresh and sweet in my mouth. May I have this dance and the next dance, and then the one after that? I am in love with these moments and I just want to hug them and freeze them in time. Oh how I smile now as I remember the first time I was really in love. It was like waking up, like part of me had been asleep until that moment, like somehow I'd been waiting for something I hadn't even known about. Remembering the past is surely God's present. All of this seems as if it were yesterday, or forever ago, in that crevasse between time and space, and I remember it all because I remember it all.

I woke up and rubbed my eyes. The mist of memories evaporated, and I looked up at the clock. Fifteen minutes had long passed. Flashing back to two weeks ago, and Karyn feeling so very sick and so darn exhausted.

The pulmonologist prescribed antibiotics and bed rest. Karyn's oxygen capacity was down to 8%, a mere 8% out of 100. I asked the doctor "How much of a window does Karyn have?" The doctor replying, "Karyn has no window."

Where the heck was that nurse? One hour. Two hours. Two and a half hours. Minutes passed so slowly they seemed sliced out of time. What is the delay? No one came to get my sister and me. I again buzzed to go back and visit. How many times was this? The ICU protocol is you pick up the phone by the old metal desk, and buzz to the main ICU charge desk, and they contact nursing. They announce your name when you are allowed to enter the ICU. Three hours. Four hours. Every minute seemed like an hour. How many times have I looked at the clock on the wall? I am back at school and see the sign by the clock in the front of the room, Time Passes Will you? Will I pass? Four hours. Seems more like four years.

The wait was excruciating. Waiting for someone does that. Minutes turned to hours to a lifetime. Time, there is a weight to it, and right now I can feel it heavy over me. I paced back and forth and looked like a man whose wife was having her first baby. And I was. My wife was being reborn. What is going on? I want to see you.

Finally, one of the nurses came out and said there had been an episode. Her tone was as delicate as a bubble of dish soap, thin, shiny and ready to pop. An "episode". "What do you mean, an episode?" My heart sped up; I could feel it knocking against my chest and hear the blood pumping in my ears. Staff were unsure if Karyn had suffered a stroke, a seizure or something else. "An episode." Her words moved through me, like fast moving thunderhead clouds transforming my landscape. Her words falling like a hard rain to the ground. Time expands when something terrible happens. Time no longer moved.

The resident doctor-in-charge, with both hands in the pockets of his long white coat came out, and looked through the door of the waiting room. "Mr. Schad, can you come out here?" The doctor corralled us and spoke to Pam and me in his calming voice. He paused, seeming to choose his words. He looked like he had just eaten something that disagreed with him. I braced myself for the smack of the newspaper. Bad news has always been like being thumped on the head by something heavy. It comes all at once, without shades or degrees. The world goes from white to black in an instant. The world divides.

One corner of his mouth curled up, as if he'd just stepped into something disgusting, "There has been an episode." If this had been a movie, this is where the needle on the record player would screech off its track. I glanced up and found his eyes full of sympathy and it was almost overwhelming. A noticeable beat before he spoke again, as if he had lost the thread of his speech. The next few moments were brittle. "We're not sure what happened but we are running tests. Karyn cannot move her entire left side. She cannot move her left arm, her left hand or her left leg. She may be placed back on the ventilator this evening." I winced like the doctor had punched me in the stomach. Fear began to avalanche inside me, gaining speed, and mass. My face is a riot of fear. Every nerve in my body is crackling and my chest will not be quiet. A scorching ache bubbled back up inside of me, pain searing my chest. I have a million questions I want to ask. I have a million worries caught inside me.

We think and hope that doctors "know" everything, but actually doctors are people like us. Many, many things we want them to know, just because we want them to know. It does not happen; it does not work that way. Doctors are not as powerful as we wish them to be. We wish them to be almighty because our life depends on them. Please doctors help my wife to be my wife.

My head swiveled from doctor to nurses. Pam and I had been looking forward so much to seeing Karyn breathing on room air. A searing pain clawed through me. This was a Disney movie gone haywire. Pam and I trudged back to Karyn's cubicle. That day, those steps became the longest forty feet a man walks in such a short time.

Karyn was working to focus on us; a deer in the headlights had more expression. My wife looked powerless and scared, so confused, and I felt my heart somersault in my chest. Her eyes would widen suddenly, then droop down, then widen suddenly and dart around the room, a haunted look. She was swimming through cloudy water, not able to see clearly. Her head turning like an antenna trying to find a signal. Sadly, someone had hit the dimmer switch and turned down her whole being.

Mostly, I remember her eyes, unusually wide open and intense and staring hard, directly at me, and yet seemingly without comprehension. Her eyes sunk deep into their darkened sockets, like a prisoner of war, a prisoner of her own war. Her wonderful grin began to look pasted on her face; she had become her own shadow.

Pam stood sentinel on the right side of the bed, and I took my wife's left hand into my hand. I was holding her hand but she did not realize it. I grasped her hand, and held it next to our bodies, a bridge between her heart and my heart. Her hand and arm were limp. I held her hand for I feared if I let go, she would drift away. I felt her drifting away, like ice on a sea. I just wanted Karyn to come back to me. Karyn tried to send a message to her left arm, but her brain sent it back: return to sender, sorry no such address.

I swallowed the lump in my throat and tried to sound normal. "Hi," and Karyn responded back with a puzzled, "Hi". She stared blankly out, no expressions of sadness or worry or surprise. Pain leaked out through the cracks in my voice. My jaw trembled and I asked, "How are you?" and Karyn replied with a one word answer, "Okay." Her eyes blinking, struggling to focus. My voice quavered and I cleared my throat. I asked Karyn what my name was, and Karyn could not answer. Karyn did not know my name. My wife could not tell me who I was. I swallowed hard blinking back tears. Words became my tears. Stick and stones and disease can break bones, but words kill. Me. Without.

My heart froze and a lump of coal formed in my throat. I looked down at my hands, my brow furrowed; I am struggling with how to say something. The lumps are choking off my throat. I could not draw enough breath to make a sound. There are so many words, but no words for what I am seeing, for what I am feeling.

Finally words spill out of me that I manage to squeeze through the narrow opening in my airways, "Karyn, who am I? And Karyn did not know I was her husband. She did not know my name. I pretended I did not feel like my heart was breaking. I shut my eyes for a moment, willing it away. Time slowed, something shifted in the room. I swallowed an anguished scream. The words burned leaving my mouth, "What do you see when you look at me?" "Butterflies," was the one-word reply. I felt my soul slipping away and I had to take deep breaths and put my hand over my mouth. I could feel all the steel come out of my shoulders. The air felt so heavy, my throat felt like it was closing. The air tasted so heavy and thick, I could hardly take it in.

Vast gaps between her tiny islands of memory, and an emptiness. Her memory gone, evaporated, as if it had never existed. I felt my wife, my life, being erased. Her memories swimming like little fish that she snatches at, and they wriggle out of her grasp.

An earthquake cry shuddered my entire body. I gripped fistfuls of sheet fabric to keep from falling off the edge of the earth. My body quaked for what seemed like an eternity. Tears welled in my eyes, and hot tears burned my cheeks. My eyes squeezed shut, my knuckles white. I bit my bottom lip so hard I thought it would bleed. Things are coming apart inside me, tearing loose from their foundations and scraping my innards as they fall. I was using every muscle to hide my heart break. My heart had broken, had broken for my wife.

I was falling fast without a parachute, so quickly no one could catch me. It was horrible asking these questions. Worse than horrible. I felt like I was chewing nails with each question, and more nails were being forced into my mouth.

Her face, a confused choppy mass of half-remembered feelings, insubstantial and slippery, gone before she could even attempt to name them. Her mind trying to reach her memories, but it flutters away, like ashes caught in a breeze.

Her face and eyes roaming the room, looking for a signal, like trying to find CNN in rural Albania. Why can't the doctors just transplant her memories back in her head? Don't we have neat index cards for our brain? Karyn, the love of my life, don't you know I am your husband? I am falling, and there is no bottom.

I shook and shook. Am I moving or has the entire hospital come unhinged? Struggling to regain my composure, I grasped to be strong and calm for Karyn. No questions came from my wife, my love, my cubby. Karyn only responded with one word answers to my questions. Karyn cried out in pain, "I want my mommy," who had passed away more than thirty years ago.

Waves of hurt crashed into me again and again. Karyn was not the only one that had been run over by a freight train. Make that two trains. I felt a thousand eyes on me. New lungs abound in the ICU cubicles around me, but no one is breathing.

The ICU visiting hours end at 9, and as we were leaving for the evening, I asked Karyn. "Who she wanted to send her kisses to?" Avah, our grand daughter, almost 1 1/2, was her one word answer. "Who else Karyn besides Avah? Devon" (our son)? Carly (our daughter)?" "Just Avah" her pointed reply dripped venom. Her words sharp as razor wire. A bite to her tone. Karyn sent me a chilly glare that could end global warming. Does she not know our children? More waves crash into me and I am drowning. I can't catch my breath like I am being held underwater. The only memory to float to the surface of her mind was Avah.

No one has said any of the usual things: She'll be just fine or Don't worry or She'll be better soon. Tidal waves of dread pound me. My face grows hot as the knowledge explodes inside of me like dynamite. Devastated. I said "Goodbye and I love you." I hugged her good-bye as if I was leaving for a two year stint in Afghanistan. As I turned to leave, I saw tears in the eyes of one of the nurses.

How do people breathe in these situations? Passing a mirror, I looked like I had been hit by a wrecking ball. I want to hurl a building at God. I take a breath and exhale with enough force to blow the paint off the walls. How do people function when they feel like this? My stomach is churning, roiling. I took a deep breath and another deep breath and exhaled a tornado.

I drove home feeling strange, like I'd somehow lost part of myself, like somehow part of me was still with her. My thoughts are steering me right into the mental breakdown lane. I felt weak and shaky as if I had just stepped off a roller coaster.

That evening was the longest of my life. The sky drew a black curtain, the moon hanging silver in the sky. Like Pig Pen from the Charlie Brown comic strip, my cloud hovered over me, dark and daunting, and devoid of any silver lining.

I was foolish to try to sleep. I tossed and turned and turned and tossed. My brain raced madly changing gears so rapidly that I could not hold onto a thought long enough to examine it. I breathed deeply, taking in great gulps of air, to get enough oxygen to my brain, to fend off paralyzing images. The taste was bitter. Thoughts kept swirling in my mind, faster and faster. I want to stop them but I cannot.

Magic Eight Ball, will it ever get better? I guess that for today, the answer is still No, Not yet. Magic Eight Ball says, answer hazy, ask again later.

Will it ever get better? It better.

My wife did not know who I was. My wife's life was being erased. My wife did not know she had had a lung transplant and that she could breathe on room air. A miracle had happened, and Karyn could not appreciate that after nine years living with the aid of supplemental oxygen, she could once again breathe. I am so very, very sad.

Feelings were deep and clear. Sorrow. Regret. Blame. Anger. Helplessness. All taking their separate turns to advance and retreat and then advance again, holding hands in varying combinations, but the most powerful feeling of all was one without a name and therefore unspeakable, a recognition of having lost forever someone singular and irreplaceable and beyond valuation.

The pain in my head was crippling. I fought with myself the entire night. Karyn could breathe but I could not catch my breath. Her name pulses in my head like a heartbeat.

All my thoughts were having their own conversations. What would I do? How can I get through the rehabilitation process when Karyn has suffered a stroke? Karyn, oh Karyn, what can I do? What should I do? Like dominoes, one thought triggered one into another and into another and another. How will I handle work? How can we get through this? Can we? How can I build a bridge to where she went?

Grief rose and spilled. Sobs jolted my frame. Crocodile, hot tears burned my cheeks. A fire blazed in my stomach, a pit in my stomach a mile deep. I sat up in bed and hugged myself, and the pillows were wet with tears. I would give anything to have her dry my tears. Forever I will share my thoughts and feelings with her. Forever, except for right now, and right now, I really need her.

Karyn is everywhere with me, yet she is not. I burrowed around in the sheets until I became wrapped up like a mummy.

My heart aches for both of us. If only I could just put a bucket of water on the episode, like on the Wicked Witch of the West. I now understood what it meant to have a broken heart, because mine hurt, and it was hard for me to breathe feeling I was suffocating.

I picture everything I love melting away. I am tethered to Karyn and the weight of hurt is beyond unbearable. When you have everything, sadly you have everything to lose, Everything. Without Karyn, the world is smaller; without Karyn, I am smaller.

They said fifteen minutes. In 15 minutes I will see my wife breathing on room air, but everything can just change in an unnoticed moment, the blink of an eye, the remembering of times long ago, the taking of one breath. I walked around in a mirage of certainty but everything is uncertain, and fleeting and fragile. My own breath catches for a second, and I swear my heart stalls.

In so many ways, everything about life has overwhelmingly changed, but in other ways, life is exactly the same. Karyn is alive. Karyn can breathe on room oxygen. This I can handle. I stay in the dark quiet, getting my breathing under control, my life under control. The waves have stopped, the pounding is receding. This I soak in.

When life sucked in the past, Karyn was my lifeline. Karyn is the glue that holds me together. So many thoughts in the ocean of my mind, the dam breaking. So many things I'd assumed I would revisit, oblivious to the hot breath of time on the back of my neck. If only.

Why isn't there a manual to consult? Oh yeah, I remember my mother's words—there is no manual to consult, this is just life.

I finally fall asleep for an hour around 5:00 AM. I am reminded when I awake, my eyes are not just red, but puffed out, swollen, like I am back in my childhood bedroom, waking up from a nightmare, or after seeing *Old Yeller*. But, there is no nightmare; it is my life, our life. The spill of morning sunlight through the cracked opening of the curtains shone on the mirror, and I looked like I had been in a nuclear blast. My eyes looked like I had mistaken cranberry juice for Visine.

Was God listening to my prayers? Maybe the answer isn't to ask for reasons why. Maybe I shouldn't be praying for all my problems to go away, but for strength and wisdom and faith to face those problems. Listen to my heart, that's God talking to me. Pray for God to guide me, and keep looking and asking questions until I know I have the answer. Finally, God answered the phone, which I reminded myself is never busy, and finally a wave of peace settled over me.

A strange calmness hugged me. I feel the tiniest of tiny things spark inside me, a little flame at the very bottom of my stomach that made me unafraid.

Time divided. The tiny space between then and now, between before and after. One of those moments like This Side and The Other Side I will remember forevermore. In that moment, I knew I could handle whatever I had to deal with. Karyn had suffered a stroke, and I would be there. By her side. By my wife's side. We would work through it. Move together as always, like a puzzle piece that fits, hand in glove, key in lock, arm in arm. There's that fit, a feeling of rightness.

Feeling afraid was awful but feeling helpless was even worse. I still felt hollow, shell-shocked, but I knew then that I could get through this no matter what. I can do this, one step at a time, one breath at a time. Things aren't as bad as they seem; the only thing I know is that they aren't as good as they should be.

I just needed to get through this day without crumbling. Better to face the scary things than run away from them. I knew that the sheer act of survival was going to take every ounce of strength I had.

Nothing else matters, but the things that truly matter, and Karyn matters most. I took a deep breath and tried to relax. I tried to dive down to calmer water. I am about to dive in, and God only knows how deep the water is.

MARY HAD A LITTLE LAMB, MY LAM NOT SO LITTLE
THIS SIDE

Dear Diary,

Looking back in time today and remembering high school, where I ran track like a gazelle, and held my breath effortlessly on a synchronized swimming team. Looking back to our honeymoon in 1971, and hiking Zion and Bryce National Park, up over 10,000 feet, and it was my husband, Richard, who could not keep up with me. I romp up the trails and I am looking back. He is gasping, holding his knees. Dancing disco every Friday night in the late 70's, dance after dance after dance, and my husband could not keep up with me. He must sit one out; even his sweat is sweating. Now I cannot even keep up with me.

Remembering, that it all started with two collapsed lungs, one in 1980 and one in 1981. The second collapse, ah that horrifying pop, and that familiar crushing sensation like a boulder on my chest. On the second pneumo, the physician smiled and said "We have good news and bad news—the good news, you are pregnant." The bad news? Your lung has collapsed."

Both pneumos were treated but the significance of each one was entirely overlooked. The real bad news splashing across my front pages would wait. I recovered from the collapses, unaware they were a symptom of something more serious.

I busted my butt exercising regularly, but still I complained to my doctor that I could not breathe when I worked out. The harder I worked out, the further I got behind. I was diagnosed with exercise-induced asthma and prescribed inhalers to keep down inflammation in my lungs. Despite the use of my inhalers, my symptoms gradually worsened until even walking caused me to feel out of breath and my heart beat ever-so-quickly.

My doctor performed a stress test on my heart, which showed my heart functioning well, but the pulse-oxygen monitor revealed the levels of oxygen in my blood were abnormally low. The medical staff decided the monitor must be malfunctioning. The doctors could not put two and two together.

I remember when the bottom fell out. It was 1999, and on a mountain trip with friends, I could not walk from the car to their home. What is wrong with me? Why can't I breathe? Am I broken? My doctor sent me to a pulmonologist, who ordered one CT scan, and then another CT scan. The tests showed a honeycomb of cysts where there should have been healthy lung tissue. The doctor checked my medical records and discovered the lung collapses, and an earlier surgery to remove a tumor on my kidney. Two and two was being added—4 ME.

It was a late Friday afternoon in June, when I was diagnosed. Life changed in the blink of an eye. Everything is fine until it isn't. There should have been a warning flare of danger. The doctor, rolled his stool closer to us, his face wrinkled and spasmed, as if he had just been bitten by a mosquito, and said to me, "Karyn, do you know what LAM is?" And I responded with a look, only I own, "If I say no, can I have something else?" The doctor kept talking, "I have heard about LAM. I have only read about LAM but I have never met a woman who has LAM."

My future was folding in on itself. We are not meant to be able to see into our future. I had been feeling breathless for a while. But it was only after many years, that I sought out doctor after doctor. I had felt a little breathless, especially going uphill and climbing stairs, and riding a bicycle, but I thought that was normal. A person can lose up to 50 per cent of lung capacity without noticing much change. I think my active life masked my breathlessness, as my muscles were efficient and I was not overweight. The more I tried, there just was no improvement.

We never see the ambush coming, do we? That "You have LAM," "You have a lung disease" moment that pops the bubble. "You have LAM." Words that can change a world.

The doctor had me at "Dying." I wept, feeling all my rage, confusion and grief pour out of me in one mighty rush. I could have drowned in my tears. Hurt was stamped on my face. The doctor left Richard and me in the room alone, and each time he returned I was crying. My thoughts roamed to my mother, who had died of a brain tumor, of cancer, at age 52. I had always feared I would die at the same age.

The doctor put a period at the end of a sentence that wasn't supposed to have ended yet. That Friday I was told I had ten years to live, and that there was no treatment. My heart pounded; my brain screamed out in disbelief. I went from thinking there was something a little wrong with my lungs to thinking I am going to die within the next 10 years.

There was no cure. LAM. I spat the words out of my mouth like poison. My only hope was a lung transplant. The doctor's words ached like a sucker punch. Maybe it's more of a stab. Whatever it is, it hurts. Whoosh, I felt the air go out of my stomach and the room. Whoosh. I can feel something inside of me unraveling, like the release of a helium-filled balloon. Can't someone fix it? Can't someone make it go away?

I should have put both my hands up in the air. I was being robbed of my innocence by LAM and lung disease.

We sat in silence after the diagnosis as several eons passed. I'll never forget this moment; it's time-stamped in my memory. Neither of us said a word. Neither of us had to. I looked at my husband and for a moment, I was drawn into his soul. I could see everything; the depth of his sorrow, his anger, his despair. I listened to the doctor in a daze of shocked misery. I had gone to a dark place on a moonless night in some creepy horror movie, and Richard and I are parked on a secluded rood, and then I hear a twig branch break. LAM.

God, life needs a fast-forward button, because there are days and moments you just don't want to have to live through, not again, but they keep coming around and I am powerless to stop time or speed it up or do anything to keep from having to face it. How can I continue to put one foot in front of the other when my breath is being taken away? How can I smile and talk and just be, like I am the old me, like nothing has changed? But it all has. Ten years. How do I measure my life in time? Do I now measure it in days, weeks, months, years?

When I first heard the diagnosis, I wanted to know how long I have, how much of a life I still have ahead of me. When a limit was placed on my life, when all of a sudden life seemed more urgent, I just wanted to know how long. How long do I have? How long?

I was the 200th woman in the world diagnosed with LAM. My husband was right. I am one of a kind.

What the heck was this stupid LAM? This LAM; it was like trying to picture a color in a Crayola Box I had never ever seen. Darn it, I don't won't to be a case.

Was a lung transplant, my only hope? C'mon. I believed I would never get to the point of needing a double lung transplant, but by 2001, I went through evaluation for transplant, knowing it was not going to be necessary. But I was proven wrong.

My ten years are almost up. Now I can barely breathe and I sleep all the time. I have been active on the transplant list at the University of Colorado hospital for almost two and a half years, with no calls, and I am waiting and waiting and I am dying. I have become my own shadow.

Accepting the death sentence of a lung disease is like falling down a flight of stairs in slow motion—I take it one bruise at a time, a blow, a landing, another short descent. I am not able to run or walk. Bump. I am not able to play or walk with my granddaughter or my dogs. Ouch. Not being able. Black and blue. Thinking about what is gone is the pain. I muttered to myself, "Nothing," which was odd, because it was everything.

After diagnosis, I would move for months as if I was underwater. Which is scarier? What is imagined or what is real? Oh my God, how am I going to get through this? It was like being in that horror nightmare and thinking I will wake up, and everything will be fine, but it wasn't a nightmare, and I did not wake up. Shock, panic, paralysis. I cried and cried and cried some more. I had mini-breakdowns over the next several months where I curled up in bed for days-on-end and retreated from the realities of my world. I was trying to outrun the heartache that was chasing me down. If only. If only. The regrets vibrated to the rhythm of my pounding heart. If only, an anchoring beat. The chorus drummed in my head over and over again, an anchoring beat for the chirping fears and incessant what-ifs that flew through my head like scattered birdsong. Finally, I focused on what I could do, not what I could not do. You know what they say about hitting yourself over the head with a hammer—it feels so good when you stop. I can't exist sitting in my house on my butt feeling sorry for myself. For the first time in a very long, long time, the LAM was not everything.

I had gone to a very dark place, and it took a while for my eyes to adjust, but then I saw things, things I never saw before. This isn't what my life is supposed to be about or is it? We all know death is coming, and we all have the chance to make the most of our time; to choose how we spend our days. There is a limit to our days, it's not a secret.

I learned eventually that there is no answer to how long—those predictions and prognoses do not mean everything. The doctors, "they" do not know for sure when my "use by date" will come. Time's surface is slick as oil, and there is just no way, no matter how hard I try, to hold onto it. What's most important is my living, not the preparing to die. I remind myself of that each and every day, of the living, no matter how much time I have left.

When you are faced with a serious illness, you can let it take over your life, or you can learn to co-exist with it, to make peace with how things are. There is nothing you can do about a situation that is intolerable but tolerate it. I have this horrible dream that I am doing dishes and the phone rings, and my husband answers it, and hands the phone to me. It's for you, it's LAM. Maybe, I should have said, I'm busy with life, don't call back.

Having LAM made me feel at first like I was a failure, and I was not used to failing at anything. When I finally admitted defeat, and outed myself as a LAMMIE, and put on my oxygen, I felt like I had won. Denial is a wonderful thing, for a short time, but I can't stay there too long. Denial is not part of my future. Let me be clear diary—acceptance of LAM and liking it are different: I do not have to like it. I do not like it.

Normal is gone. It's out the window along with the air. There is no normal after diagnosis. Perhaps there never was. Diary, this does not mean I am abnormal;

no one with LAM or a lung disease is abnormal. But in my new normal, I am not giving up. I am just trying to accept something I have to accept.

I felt like I was being betrayed by my body. I am not LAM but I have become my LAM. It owns me, defines me. What stage? Are you desaturating? Pre—or Post Transplant-? How many pneumos? What's your FEV1? The dreaded How Longs?

I wanted a life busy with things other than LAM, but I am on the LAM merry-go-round. I have learned about a new world full of oxygen and pills and PFT tests, not to mention a whole new vocabulary of LAM Speak.

I know my LAM is here. The holes are in my lungs and the LAM continues to spread. I know the LAM is taking away part of me each day. I know that the ticking-down of LAM is a death sentence, for a crime I did not commit.

LAM is a specter that lives in my mind just as the cells live in my lungs and lay claim there. The clock is tolling midnight.

Women, like me, who have LAM can champion the cause and talk of what could be. Women who do not have the disease can champion the cause and talk of what should be. All of us can champion the cause and tell of what must be.

I'll write soon,

Karyn

LAM—A Breath-Taking Challenge
Both Sides

LAM, or lymphangioleiomyomatosis, is a progressive and frequently fatal lung disease, that affects only women, usually in their child-bearing years. Lymphangioleiomyatosis is pronounced limf-an-gee-o-ly-o-my-o-ma-to-sis. "Lymph" refers to the lymph vessels and "angio" refers to the blood vessels. "Leiomy" means smooth muscle, "oma" is a tumor, and "tosis" refers to a disease condition. LAM, the gentle sounding acronym, sounds so nice like Mary has a little. But it is anything but little.

More than 1500 women with LAM have now been identified (which is virtually nil in the world of disease statistics)—consider then each week about 1500 people die from Alzheimer's and each day 1500 people die from cancer. Scientists do estimate that approximately 250,000 women with LAM are going misdiagnosed or undiagnosed. LAM is rare affecting only just five women in every million people.

The diagnosis of LAM can be difficult because many of the early symptoms are similar to those of other lung diseases, such as asthma, emphysema, or bronchitis.

A normal lung is solid, while in a LAM lung, there are air cysts ("blebs") or fluid filled cysts, little tiny holes, so the lung looks like Swiss cheese. More and more cysts invade, growing uncontrollably, filling up the lungs until there is no more healthy tissue. The LAM cells destroy the delicate architecture of the lung tissue and replace it with more and more cysts. The cysts and clusters grow throughout the lung and begin to block and choke off airways. LAM prevents air from moving freely out of the lungs, preventing adequate amounts of oxygen from reaching the body's organs.

LAM's abnormal smooth muscle growth slowly smothers the lungs and closes off the respiratory passages.

Most commonly, women with LAM will experience shortness of breath after physical exertion, and over time, women may find that they have trouble breathing even at rest. Other symptoms include a bad cough and chest pain, which can be a sign of a collapsed lung (pneumothorax), which a majority of women with LAM will experience, one or more times, in one or both lungs. Karyn's lung collapsed twice. A lung is at risk of collapsing when air escapes or leaks into the chest cavity. This build-up of air creates pressure, which in turn causes the lung to collapse, preventing it from filling up with air properly. Beyond making it difficult to breathe, the collapse can cause the heart and major blood vessels to be pushed to the unaffected part of the chest, which can dangerously lower blood pressure levels.

Women with LAM are at risk of lymph fluid leaking into their chests, and enlarged lymph nodes. In addition, because LAM surfaces mostly in women, doctors think that estrogen plays a role, and in some cases, women are advised not to become pregnant. Karyn's second lung collapse came at the same time she became pregnant.

LAM women are also at risk of developing benign kidney tumors (angiomyolipomas). Karyn had a benign tumor removed from her kidney in 1991.

The rate of progression and the incidence of resulting symptoms can and does vary considerably among patients.

All races are affected and women with LAM have been identified in over sixty countries. The average age of women at the time of diagnosis is approximately forty-eight, though, at the time of diagnosis, the reported age varies from six to seventy-five years of age. (Karyn was 49). Also, most women with LAM have had symptoms for three to five years before ultimately being diagnosed. (Karyn's first lung collapse was in 1980).

LAM is a progressive disease that at this time cannot be cured, is caused by a genetic mutation, sometimes inherited, sometimes random, which eventually consumes the lungs. Lung transplantation is often considered as a last resort. While many women with LAM add several years to their lives through transplantation, it is not a cure. Karyn was transplanted May 17, 2009.

Dear Diary,

With LAM, my lungs plain suck at being lungs. Breathing with LAM is like trying to pull air through swollen tubes. One day I was fine. Then I was sucking air through a straw and now . . . Have you ever tried sucking air through a cocktail straw? LAM is not like cancer with stages marking the decline. But if it was, the fourth stage has left the depot.

Karyn

AM I MY GENES? LAM CAME UNINVITED, UNWANTED
THIS SIDE

Dear Diary,

You just take some things for granted, like the love of your husband and your children, the sun rising tomorrow, and the breathing of fresh air from your lungs.

Once I crossed over into LAM world in 1999, I became a stranger in a strange world. Nothing, not anything, no longer, is taken for granted. What to expect, what to hope for, what to fear—none of those are clear. I knew the day LAM came in uninvited and unwanted, my world was going to change. I had crossed a line and there was no going back. Life back on Planet Earth will never ever be the same.

I remember one day walking, weighted down by an anchor masquerading as an oxygen tank, and kids chirping at me, that I shouldn't have smoked. I wanted to yell back, smoking never caused this. Smoking in no way causes LAM, but, rather than argue with those pointing fingers at me, I would point back and say, rather calmly and sternly, "And don't you start!" There can be some good from the bad LAM.

I remember how the simplest task became difficult and complicated. For us Lammies, we become no longer self-sufficient. I can no longer do whatever I want, and how I want. My arms and legs are missing that little oomph that will put me on my feet. I sit back down, gather my strength, and go for it again. Scary because I know sooner or later, I may not be able to make that second try. I am becoming a turtle on its back. I am becoming inert, as unmoving as a portrait.

I cannot change reality. My illness is here to stay. My pills and medications are here to stay. My lungs will fight me every day. Cultivating well-being is an ongoing process of learning to accept my limitations. I am tired of being tired.

Stairs used to lead to somewhere interesting, or important. Now, the stairs go nowhere. Slight inclines have become hills. I climb stairs and my chest moves up and down as if I have climbed a Fourteener. I think twice, three times, before going outside to retrieve the letters from the mail box. Groceries are no longer carried. My LAM belongs to me alone and separates me from the people, the healthy ones, who do not even notice they are healthy.

When you have LAM, you should get a pass on life's other problems, but, of course, it does not work that way. Life goes on and I must participate. The same old problems exist, along with new ones I could never imagine. And the problems from the past just do not go away. It's hard to sort through it all, but I really have no choice. Maybe having LAM means you just have to work harder to get things done.

I remember back to the spring of 2008 when I was no longer able to take showers, another little loss of self-sufficiency and control. A loss of freedom that the LAM has caused and I hated it. It scared me also, how far will IT go? How much of my strength will the LAM steal? I know women who could not get off a couch. Will I end up bed-ridden?

So it gets harder and harder to do the same things. And I would say, "I think I can do it, work a little harder to do them, and make the LAM work harder to try and stop me." Like the late night commercials, "But, wait there's more." The worst? When I realized I could no longer care for my granddaughter, Avah. All I could do was place her on the floor surrounded by her toys. I could no longer pick her up and hold her. Her little arms would reach up towards me. And all my lungs could do was cry.

My world had shrunk to the size of my withered lungs. The only thing expanding in my life was my medical file, which looked like the Los Angeles telephone directory. In my shrunken life, all I could do was sit, eat, and sleep.

If you were not there at the bad moments, if you were not there to agonize over another sign of deterioration, then you could not see how I had changed, but I could. You get used to a stage of illness and then suddenly it gets worse and your world shrinks further.

Everyone needs to feel that they have some control over their own life. We all do. I hate feeling helpless; getting sicker. My lungs feel like a sack of cement. I hate that I am suffocating. Please someone cauterize the ache of loss. LAM turns off the lights, one by one, and it was getting darker.

LAM turned my world upside down, shook it hard, and then looked to see what was left. LAM came knocking, I didn't want it, but it barged in, uninvited, unwelcome. I wish I could make the disease go away; maybe I could chase LAM into a corner, push it off a cliff a long distance away, or just get it out of my consciousness and allow me something else to think about, but I never forget that I have LAM. I cannot feel them but I know there are holes in my lungs.

It is easier to have LAM than to pretend I do not have LAM. When I admitted defeat, I felt like I had won. Denial is not shoes I walk in for long—life is way too short to spend a lot of time there.

LAM is a part of my life now. I never forget that I have LAM. It will always be a part of me. It's a part of who I am. LAM is only a small part of who and what I am; never the sum total. I can live with that. My LAM has humbled me. I have learned so much, been given so much; to forget that I have LAM would be to forget part of who I am. I am a LAMMIE.

I am not my LAM but none of us are who we are before we got sick and sometimes that's so hard for me to accept since it is not a change I welcomed. LAM may be another adjective to describe me, but it is not who I am. It is one of the things I have, but it is not who I am. It is not who I am. It is not. LAM's trying to kill me. I'm trying to stop it from doing that. Most days that seems to be enough to say about LAM. The world is full of far more interesting things.

Don't they always say in movies you should never show fear? I do not want the LAM to know that I am worried about it. I want the LAM to be worried about what I am going to do to it; for all that the disease has done to me. I hope that LAM lies awake at night worrying about what I am going to do to it next. That only seems fair.

I know LAM is there. I know it is taking away part of me each day. Some days, I want it just to go away. Some days, I want it just to be quiet. But LAM is never quiet, always trying to find a place to cause trouble.

I want to scare LAM like a vampire caught out at sunrise running like hell toward the safety of a hidden coffin in a windowless basement. LAM, I hope you are getting tired and frustrated. I hope LAM is thinking about all the bad things it has done, because I am going to make it work to get me.

Lung disease can be unrelenting. Boxers get breaks between rounds. Football players catch their breath in a huddle. A few seconds can make all the difference in the world, between victory and defeat. I just need a timeout, but there are no timeouts with LAM.

Diary, it's not the pain. It's not the fear, the uncertainty, or the anger. It's the stress that's the toughest to deal with sometimes. I can take the medication for the pain or discomfort. I talk to my friends about the fear; I remind myself I am not alone. When the anger flares, I remind myself that there is no one to be angry at. It doesn't mean that those feelings are not valid and oh so strong; they are, but what they add up to is stress—the pressure of coping with everything that LAM brings with it can feel like a vise, and sadly, there's not an easy answer as to how to deal with the stress. Everyone around me, my husband, the caregivers, my family, my friends, my doctors—they all fall victim to it.

What would help, would be some sort of break? A short recess? But there are no breaks in LAM world. Being a LAMMIE is hard work. I'm on the job 24/7. I am tired, physically tired, mentally tired. I don't get weekends off or holidays off. If I don't feel like it physically, I live with it mentally. Having LAM just plum tuckers me out; it wears down my soul.

LAM is all—consuming fatigue, bone-deep, non-negotiable, elusive and ever-present. Sometimes I try to fight it and plow my way through, but usually try as I might, the fatigue is larger than I am. It is not sleepiness; it is exhaustion. I remind myself I am working harder just to be alive than most people ever work in their whole life while doing things; just staying alive is all-consuming. Brushing my teeth makes my heart race at 150 beats a minute. Tethered to an oxygen tube connected to a tank in our utility room, my umbilicus. Trudging upstairs with my tank, I have to stop every three steps up the stairs to our bedroom. The muscles in my arms and legs screaming for oxygen. I am suffocating. Will I always feel like I am walking through mud?

LAM is drowning in slow motion. Each time I stopped on the stairs, I gasped for breath, felt woozy, and ever-so-tired, and out of breath. I can't get enough air. I can no longer taste the air. If only wishes could come true, my lungs wouldn't ache as if all the space inside them is used up.

Climbing to the second floor is like Mount Everest for me. My lungs feel like they'll burst. My mobility has been stolen. If I leave my glasses upstairs when I come downstairs in the morning, they stay there until my husband comes home. I only have enough oomph to make it up the stairs once a day.

One day I was climbing mountains in Utah, and now I am suffocating. Lung disease has drank away muscles on my bones. My lung scans look like a little kid had been set free with a can of black paint inside my lungs.

I look into the mirror unable to recognize the person I once was. A short walk from the bedroom to the bathroom leaves me panting, grabbing onto the counter to catch my breath. The light above the mirror shines on my face, pale and sunken with fatigue. Dark circles surround my eyes like runny mascara.

I tell myself in the mirror that no matter how each day goes, I win, the LAM wins, or it's a draw. I can get through it, for another day. I am after all a LAMMIE.

People treat me differently, like LAM is contagious, like I have been hit by a whole ton of bad luck and they don't want it dumped on them. LAM isn't contagious, but attitudes surely are. My LAM forced me to make a decision whether to live in fear for the rest of my life, or embrace the life I have. I chose to embrace life, spar with the demon, and live as best as I can.

I can choose to give in to depression, or I can say, this is my life and I'm going to live it as best I can. Life just doesn't wait. If I stand still, life passes me by, and it may be too late.

LAM is a future that is uncertain and difficult. There are options in fighting LAM, but going it alone is not one of them. LAM is an unchartered road, and who knows where it will take me. There is but one certainty; that I cannot get through it alone. I need others and they need me. In the darkness of the dark, my sister LAMMIES and the LAM Foundation brought me hope and in the world of LAMMIES, running at the speed of life, that's a very, very big thing. LAMMIES and the LAM Foundation are my cushioning like I am inside a big bouncy house, and no matter how hard I hit the wall, I'll just rebound.

LAM changed my calendar. I go by days, and I take them one day at a time. Everything changed that one day, the day I figured out there was exactly enough time for all the important things in my life. I do not live my life worrying about the "What Ifs" for if I did that, I would never enjoy the "What's Happenings."

I am conscious of the passing of time, the turning of the wheel. After all, time is so very precious to all us LAMMIES. It is our currency. This oxygen tank on my back and the cannulas in my nose, make people stare and children rant, will buy me more time. What more do I need to hear?

LAM made me realize how precious each day can be and how important it is to appreciate them all. That does not mean that every day is going to be a good day and when I say I try to live each day to the fullest, that can mean just about anything. Sometimes just making it downstairs to the chair is enough to make it a good day. So I guess today was a good day.

Sometimes, I feel I need to say something, each day, something worthwhile. But sometimes, all I have really to say is, "Hey made it through another day." That's not very profound or even thoughtful, but it is the over-riding truth of the day. Even though I know the beast of LAM is lurking near me all the time, today belonged to me, not the Beast. Today is my day. How I love to say today.

To love a LAMMIE, my husband, I know, is in turn to feel sad, frightened, concerned, angry, lost, and often helpless, and you do all this for the most part silently. Does it help you to know that I understand this? My fighting LAM is like a giant game of Mother May I—it sometimes seems as if I take one step forward, only to take two steps back. I get out of breath and become bluer than normal, not that it's normal to turn blue, but for me, it's normal. Ah, wouldn't it be great to go back to my old normal, not LAM normal, for a little while?

Do the people who know I have LAM ever forget? How do others look at me? And when they do, is the LAM all they see? Do they look at me like I'm the bearded lady in the circus? Am I LAM girl? I am the trapeze artist in pink tights holding the spotlight above the crowd. Am I like the kids in high school known by one single, dominant feature? The Tall Guy, the Brain, the Jock, the Fat Girl. Do they ever see me the way I used to be, just a normal person? Do we ever see ourselves the way we used to? Can we ever step back into our own lives, even for a short time? My mind may let me, but my body has a habit of reminding me that just is not the case. Normal Karyn is something I was; but that is over.

I know that I was careless with life. I walked around in a mirage of certainty, but everything is uncertain and fleeting and fragile. I wonder to myself all the time if I can ever get back the "me" that I once had. As I travel down the road, the experiences change me without me even knowing it until suddenly I see a reflection of myself and I don't realize it's me I am seeing. Maybe the new normal is better than the old normal, because now I truly know that each day is so very important, and how much I appreciate all the good days and the oh-so-good-moments.

LAM altered my body, my mind, my feelings, my expectations, my dreams. Altered but not destroyed. The Road Not Taken has become the Road Taken.

I heard a person today wishing for some excitement in their boring lives. Now sometimes I wish for a boring life. Sometimes it takes something like this to let you know how wonderful a normal life, a boring life is. Sometimes I hear the clock ticking down on my life. This new normal, sometimes it stinks. But I have the air freshener out. There is no normal after diagnosis. Perhaps there never was.

I may look the same, I may sound the same. I do wake up every morning knowing that I have been given another day and sometimes that's just enough.

I would love not to be breathless. I do remember what it felt like to run and play and climb and hike. I miss my old normal, my new normal is something I do the best I can with each day. I guess a part of my old normal was living with a sense of security that I never had a right to. LAM stole a part of my life I will never get back. LAM stole control over my life. I was the master of my own identity, master no longer. Maybe I was just arrogant in thinking I was in control.

LAM is not punishment for my cheating on that US History test in the 11th grade. LAM is an indiscriminate killer and LAM just does not care who you are, or what you have done, whether you are a good person or a bad person, or I suspect a little bit of both. LAM comes when it wants to—maybe that is why it just seems so darn cruel.

LAM does not care who you are. LAM does not care if you are young and pregnant. LAM does not care if you are poor or wealthy. LAM does not care if you are black or white or brown or pink. LAM does not care. It's up to us to care.

I do get angry. God, do I get angry. Those feelings of "It's just not fair" or "Why me" come welling up inside. Who or what do I get angry at? The LAM does not care. Anger is so darn satisfying that you can forget it's actually useless. Although it would be fun to think the little germy cells could feel my anger. I think more often than not, I feel frustrated. I can't do the things I used to do—I feel crappy and my body has changed, my life has changed, and it just shouldn't be this way but it is. It is, and anger or frustration, sadly do not help much.

I do struggle with the whys in life. Why her? Why him? Why me? I know there's no good answer. I get so darn frustrated with the things that are out of my control, and I wonder why people do not deal with the things they can control.

LAM came knocking. Didn't want it, but it barged in, uninvited, unwelcome. Maybe there was a why and maybe not. It didn't really matter. Today I breathe and I am living with, not dying of LAM, even though my lungs are an absence, empty as a zero, a spot of nothing in the air.

I have LAM but I never forget that LAM does not have me. I live for the day, the moment and the fact that I am here today and that bus did not hit me while crossing the street.

I treasure that what is now will never be again.

I am a LAMMIE, and I made it through today. Let's see what tomorrow will be like,

Karyn

BUT YOU LOOK SO GOOD
THIS SIDE

Some people had a hard time dealing with Karyn's illness as she became more frail, so they opted to stay away. People did not know what to say or do, or how to act, so they avoided Karyn. Our world sadly does not want to deal with sickness. The rules change when you have a chronic illness. You are an outsider to the healthy world, an offensive reminder of the ugly underbelly of life.

Some people avoid disease; discourage disease, as if it were shameful. For them, it was easier to pretend her disease and her deteriorating health did not exist. These people internalized their air-brushed version of Karyn's reality. They pretended not to see what they saw. They remained convinced that the best policy was to treat disease and Karyn like a stray dog, as long as you did not make eye contact, the dog, Karyn, the disease would eventually go away.

When people found out about Karyn's medical condition, they often said, "BUT YOU LOOK SO GOOD." I was never sure what they meant. I assume part of it has to do with confusion. They did not understand how someone that looks good can be sick because they were so focused on visual cues; whether Karyn looked pale or gray or tired. Some people were so focused on the visual cues that they thought Karyn was exaggerating about her condition, "Well if I cannot see it, then it must not exist." "You must be getting better." As both of us said many times, "LAM is a progressive chronic disease—you never get better, you only get worse."

So many people said to me "She looks so good." She is not, but I repeat it back to them, that "Yes, she does look good." This is how some deal with sickness. They establish a new standard and embrace it with manufactured cheer, as if the epic nature of life and death, of LAM, of lung disease, could be thwarted with a veneer of breezy compliments and light conversation.

Dear Diary,

I know what it feels like to be a stranger in a strange land, to have everyone walking quiet steps around me, some investigating, some ignoring my every move. The first are seeking signs of familiarity, the second are so scared of what my experience might reveal about themselves, they prefer to keep their eyes shut. They would look at me like they were a child, and I was a Stranger, Capital S, offering candy.

Why do people want to know what I feel and then tell me that is not how I feel. I do not feel good. I know a tension can exist between how I feel and how sick I appear in the eyes of others. When people want to believe I am healthy, then logically, sort of, that becomes how I think I should feel. That constant tension is emotionally draining. I am forced to live a lie to make others feel better.

The most insincere question in the English language is the simple query, how are you?

With me, the word fine frequently exploded before I even heard the question mark. Who wants to be bothered? Illness may be a part of my life, but as with death, we too often fail to make our peace. My chronic condition became intensely private as I realized others did not really want to hear the truth and I know it is emotionally easier for someone to look at me as healthy, that I am holding my own.

For many of us in the sick world, You Look So Good, that tongue-in-cheek sentiment, is all too familiar. The meaning clear, really, you cannot look so good and be so sick. My illness is hidden. My LAM is like an iceberg, everything under the surface. Just because you cannot see it, does not make it non-existent or untrue. What did you expect? A cadaver? You look good. Why, thank you, so do a lot of serial killers. I am sick. I am not dead. I am here. I am still here. I am trying to live one day at a time. Know this, I miss my old life. I just miss life. I hate relying on other people when I used to be so independent. Just because I look good does not mean I feel good.

What people may not appreciate is how long it took me to look like this. How much effort just to run a comb through my hair or brush my teeth, and that I had to stop taking showers because I did not have the strength. (Yes, I do bathe). Or the effort just to wash my hair in order to keep up that pleasant façade of normalcy.

Sometimes, "You look so good" makes me want to slap them. Maybe that's good, the assurance that the whole world does not immediately see what my problems are. How good do I look? Distractingly, unbelievably good. It's called Sephora, honey. If you were told of all my health problems and limits, you too, would immediately take one look at me and blurt out, but Karyn you look so good. See? Everyone says it. I guess I cannot fault them, after all the people in my life must care about me, otherwise they would not keep asking me how I am doing.

Each time I see friends they always say, How are you feeling? You look good. Before I got LAM, no one ever told me I looked good.

Or when someone asks how I am feeling and I tell them I feel like total crap and they respond, "Well, you look good." I am like, that really does not make me feel any better or change the fact that I feel like I am gonna puke on your face right now. Good, because if I looked like I feel like, it would scare you to death.

But You Look So Good is, I know sometimes a way of saying "I do not believe you are sick". I know my disease is invisible. But I am not. I am not a book to be judged by its cover. I appreciate your concern, I really do, but sometimes, I wish my condition showed like a broken arm in a cast. I am not normal and I just want to be normal again. I want my upside-down world turned right. Do not cheer me up if I am having a bad day. I am entitled to it. Don't say, well at least you look good, unless you want a metal canister of oxygen hurled at your head.

You should see my CT scans for the last 10 years. Hey that's it, I will start carrying wallet-size photos of my CT scans! I can whip them out with my other photos. This is my husband Richard, my grandchild Avah, my dogs Bo and Jake, and this is my LAM.

Like anything, there is a positive side to having an invisible illness. It's up to me how much I divulge as to how I am feeling. That is a definite plus. Some days, I just do not feel like dealing with it, you know. Other days when my closest friends surround me, I feel more at ease to talk at length about my stupid disease. Sometimes I focus less on what people say (that I look so good), and focus more on helping them understand my disease.

I tried to explain to others that LAM made me really tired, but they thought I was being overly dramatic. You Look So Good may be meant as a compliment, but for those of us dealing with the extreme fatigue, and the plethora of emotions that come with a chronic disease, the comment falls short of the support I need. I face it, that my family and friends want to be helpful. I get it. But the longer I am sick, the more angry and frustrated they feel. That's just the way people approach illness. After all, I know most people get sick, then they get better. Once I was diagnosed with LAM, my friends and loved ones expected me to be treated and then get well. When this did not happen, I think they felt frustrated and angry—quite similar to the feelings I was experiencing.

My disease is unpredictable. I have LAM; it's a fact of life for me and I am learning to live with it, but I just wish my insides felt as good as my outside looks.

I wish I could tell you all this and more. I think the illusions are easier for you to live with. Let's make a deal and you can pretend I am always healthy and I can pretend I am always healthy and happy. I am sure it would work for a while. But it would really be work. Do you really care how I am feeling when you ask? There are so many things I wish people knew about me, but I won't say because you do not ask, and when you do, you are not truly listening.

A person approaches me and says But You Look so Good. As soon as I have an audience, the act starts. I've studied the lines of what I'm supposed to say, I'm doing fine or okay or some days are better than others, or as well as can be expected. Finally, I would say, "I'm great." I hate letting people see the effects of my disease. I do not care that they know I am sick, I just do not want them to have to see it or deal with it. I act like I do not care, but I do. I act like I am not scared, but I am. Pay no attention to the woman behind the smile.

I have to live my life differently from everyone else around me. I have to think about just getting out of bed. I need to think about having enough oxygen while doing errands; that normal people do not put much thought into. I worry I will leave my oxygen tank on when I am not using it, and it will be empty when I need it.

I miss my old life. I just miss life. Just because I look good does not mean I am good. Everything looks the same. Don't they know everything has changed?

I smile a lot these days. I laugh, talk with friends, to my oldest bestest friends who did not ignore me, leave me when one diagnosis followed another and my oxygen levels decreased and my smiles turned to tears and they were still there.

This is who I am and no amount of make-up will change me. Go if you want to. Leave. You were not there and now I know that. You did not care about me. You cared more about the image of a healthy person who looked so good, whose world had not yet changed.

It is dizzying, exhausting to be two different people. This is who I am, good days and bad days. Sometimes there will be days that I am funny, that you just cannot believe I am sick. Then the next day I may be that really sick girl who used to be funny. I am doing my best.

I am trying to be me.

Love, Karyn

P.S. Dear People, Just because you cannot see it, does not mean it does not exist. I am not fine, and I am not good, and I am not the same.

NAILS ON THE CHALKBOARD
OF MY SOUL
THIS SIDE

Dear Diary,

People spotted my oxygen tank and nasal cannula. No shortage of awkward conversations in which pity dripped through people's voices and eyes. They cast their eyes away as though I were the homeless begging for change. They would look, but not see me. Why? My soul was unchanged by my physical decline. Why are they talking to me so slowly and with high-pitched voices? I wonder why they cannot see the pain in my eyes.

Sadly, they ran their nails over the chalkboard of my soul. They pitied me. They had no compassion, for pity is without any compassion. When you have compassion, all human experiences are possible. There go I, but for the grace of God. Pity is a Fool, and I pity the Fool.

Each of our experiences is both unique and completely universal. Sickness and disease happen all the time, and it does, until it happens to you, and then it is something altogether different.

I pity those who lack the compassion to feel what they see, and who do not see. No shred of sympathy, empathy or understanding. Maybe I should speak to them slowly and with a high-pitched voice? Someone needs to write The Idiot's Guide to LAM.

Did I tell you about my cousin Rachel, who got LAM and dropped dead less than 2 months later? How long did they give you to live? The awful time questions—how long, how short, how often. What are you so worked up about? Hey, I had a piece of my intestine removed last year and I am just fine. It's all in your head. It's the altitude. You just need a hobby. I know exactly what you should do. I know just how you feel. Their words thrown like spears piercing my heart.

Long shaggy dog stories about someone else's lung disease, especially one with a tragic ending. I could not get them to listen to me. They hijacked my right to talk about my own personal experience and feelings. Let Rachel and the other shaggy dogs rest in peace.

Oh, is that all? I thought you had (always in whispered tones) cancer or something. You just have to learn to live with it. You're just depressed. You just need to reduce stress and make some time for yourself. It's all in your head, if you just had a positive mental attitude, you would not feel sick. You could get better if you really wanted to. You are so lucky to spend the day in bed. LAM is a blessing in disguise. An oyster needs sand to make a pearl. Sometimes we need to feel worse to get better.

Talk to me in a normal manner. How's it going rather than always asking how's my health or how often do you have to go back to the doctor. Give me the choice of sharing concerns, fears or good news about my condition. Talk to me about the ordinary; it does so matter. I am here. Please remember, I have LAM, I am not LAM. Hear me. Accept all the good and bad about me. I do know the hard part is actually doing it.

Being able to hear what I want, what I need from you, and to give that, and not to give me what you believe I should want from you. Give me time so you may hear what I am saying. Why are there so many Teflon listeners? What I say just slides right off them. Having people listen instead of telling makes me feel real. Please be there.

I have learned we can never truly know what will help and what will hurt someone with a disease, so how can I ever know what to say, or ask, or do? I suppose the simple answer is we can't. My very wise Grandpa Harmon always told me, that there is always an easy solution to every human problem, neat, sensible and wrong. I cannot know what each Lammie and Lungie needs and wants. But I have learned, we can always be sensitive.

I remember running a nail on your chalkboard when I made an ill-fated comment about the noise of your pulse-dose oxygen in the movie theater. Each time you took a breath, a noise emitted breaking the quiet. I was embarrassed by the sounds and wanted it hushed. What? Did I not want you to go to the movies? Did I not want you to breathe?

I gave an apology to you. Apologies are given, or are they? I gave an apology, but I was really asking for something; I was asking for your forgiveness, for you to make it okay for me. I know now that apologies are much harder work for the one getting one, than the one giving one. I ask for forgiveness and I am sorry.

The ignorance of the limitations of life with a chronic illness or disability hurts as much as the actual pain. I have learned I am here for you. I may not know exactly what to say or do, and if I mess up (again), I apologize in advance and I hope you forgive me. But I want you to know how much you mean to me.

Tell me, "I am so sorry this has happened to you." Tell me, "If you ever feel like talking, I am here to listen, just listen. Please let me know what I can do to help, and can I drop off dinner for you guys next Tuesday night? Be positive. Tell me I am an inspiration. Tell me, "It is wonderful to see you again." Tell me that you missed me (and thankfully does not elicit my wanting to bark back, "If you only knew"). Tell me, "I don't know what to say, except I'm sorry."

I have to live my life differently than everyone else around me. I have to think about just getting out of bed. I need to think about my medications. I have to plan my outings around my oxygen. Just so many little things, that normal people do not put much thought into. It is like I am living in a different world than you, and I have different issues, priorities, and a language that only we Lammies and Lungies speak.

I hate popping pills and people asking me personal health questions that I do not want to answer. I hate living up to other people's expectations of what being sick is. I hate living up to other people's expectations of what a healthy person should be. I hate thinking about how or when I might die, because for me, it might be a when day, and not a someday. I hate never feeling good enough, quick enough, pretty enough, or just enough. I hate that one of my husband's acquaintances referred to me as "damaged goods." I hate people who complain they envy me because I get to nap all the time. I hate it when they yammer on, making me feel that my being alone is better than this alone feeling I get around those yammerers who don't have a clue and are being utterly annoying.

Diary, you know me. I get to pick who knows the real me. I get to pick who to share my soul with. I decide who to let in. You know that I do not want a watered down life.

I live in two worlds.

Pity is for lost causes. People, I do not want your pity.

Karyn

ICU—Intensive Care for Those of Us Waiting
The Other Side

I would arrive before 9 each morning when the ICU visiting hours began, placing myself against the far wall, facing the only opening to the world, the door. I had my own little space, parked across from the door to the hallway and the cubicles of the ICU.

The ICU waiting area is a former storage room, and as such, is a small sitting room, with about 20 chairs. A TV plays on a shelf high in the corner, droning on and on, as the words in the old magazines blur by.

The door was my window to the world; I was always looking, always watching the nurses and doctors go past the door. *Ich bin ein* East Berliner watching that lucky foreigner drive his car through the Brandenburg Gate. What lies on the other side? What is going on with my wife? Is she getting better? What is happening?

You pick up the phone on the wall by the old battered metal desk in the far corner and tell the charge nurse who answers the phone, whom you want to visit and who you are and then you wait. You want the phone to buzz back quickly, giving you the feeling that all-is-clear. It may be my wife is being visited by a doctor, having a bronch or another procedure or a bath or a million things my mind roams to and then a million more.

It's been another hour and no word; that cannot be a good sign. Hurry up and wait; the long anxious watch. The doctors passing the door look weary. How strange that my world has become so small. Watching for a doctor or nurse who is treating my wife going down the hall and cajoling them into an up-date.

Watching the door was like looking at life through the tiniest of peepholes.

I am anxious and I pick up the phone again and ask to see my wife.

Then I wait for the phone to squawk back, to walk through the door, the gate, turn right ten feet and enter the ICU.

Once I enter the ICU waiting room, nothing else exists. My world became my wife, my patient, and the short intervals I can see her.

There is no visiting in the normal sense. I am a waiter, not a visitor. I wait for doctors, for news, for a visit, for other family or friends to arrive, wait for phone calls, and wait to, someday, take another full breath. I wait for the speaker by the phone to grant permission to cross the Wall.

The big lesson of the ICU is just what in life does not matter at all, the lawn getting mowed, where you went to school, what you drive, your credit rating, house size, annual income, clothes and even work. This is a room of absence and no one in ICU talks of these things. Most of what I dealt with as real stops at the door. The ICU is real life, not what I left at home or the office.

I sit across from people I have never seen before. I have seen race, class, and age differences dissolve instantly. The ICU is filled with a most generous compassion and I have watched people change diapers, go outside to change tires, share food and fears and faith with others who in any other setting might be spurned or shunned.

That's the thing about the ICU: I could talk to another person sitting next to me for hours and never know her name, and share my deepest secrets and then never see her again. We in the ICU serve each other. We take messages for each other. We fetch coffee for each other. We go out and buy food for people we have never seen before and will never see again.

A white dirt-poor woman from the North Carolina outback whose father made hillbilly pop, moonshine, converses easily with a black woman from the projects. I ask where the main surgery waiting area is and one woman says it's down yonder. I now know how far yonder is. The details of life are left outside the ICU door. There is no color here, no politics, no bias.

I sit and stare at the vacant metal desk and abandoned phone, waiting for it to chirp back my name.

In one gasp of air, one lump, one scream, one unexpected bit of blood, one stroke-like episode, priorities change. In a single morning in ICU, watching life drain and change out of someone you love. Will my wife know me? Is she off the vent? Can she move her left side?

We, the waiters, do not have to pretend all is fine. We can share dark humor. We share wisdom hewed from hard experience. We comfort each other. We help each other and that is a great comfort. We become comfortable with the uncomfortable.

No one should face the unknown by themselves. That was a great lesson, that I was not alone, that I could lean on others for help, and that I could help others when I felt weak and lost and confused. Maybe there is a dark cloud hanging over my head, but at least it's shady.

In the comfort of being together, we sit and talk of trivialities and of life and death. There are shocked looks, tears, laughter at one of my very old jokes. We hold our collective breath, all of us murmuring our prayers. We pray. Silence.

Everyone is together, each alone with our own thoughts. Compassion is heavy in the air, even heavier than my own. The pain I feel for someone sitting in the ICU room and the other waiters understanding what I am going through. We, who quietly whimper, are newborn puppies finding warmth and security in our proximity.

People of faith are thankful and offer words of gratitude and encouragement. One older very wise woman, holding her dog-eared Bible, as tears cloud her eyes and rolled down her cheeks, told me that Faith is seeing a rainbow in each tear. She is worrying her husband's old handkerchief, the initials LG barely readable in the corners, and I clutch her hand, plugging into her lifeline of strength. Her voice so soft, her eyes so very warm, with compassion as her husband of 60 years suffers through his final illness. Nothing is so strong as gentleness, nothing is as gentle as real strength.

We sit in silence. Cannot silence be just as intimate as talk? Can we not touch sometimes without words? When someone talks, we listen. Listening is a most powerful act of giving. We listen each other into being. There is no reason to suffer alone when we can suffer together.

I see another patient's husband, an old friend, come into ICU, "How are you doing today? I know this is hard and I hope the best for you. You are in my thoughts and prayers." Amen to that child. We hug.

I give out many hugs. Who would deny the power and grace of another person's touch? One reaching out to another, affirming the need we all share to have someone declare you are good enough to love. Mom said it best, a hug is the perfect gift—one size fits all and no one minds if you exchange it.

The narratives of life define the South—they look for a kind ear to talk to, not someone to solve their problems. They want someone who cares enough to give them the time to listen to their story. People here allow the narratives of life to pour out of their souls as freely as sweet tea with a twist of lemon. They talk to each other, not to get to the bottom line but to get to know each other.

It's been another hour and no word; that cannot be good sign.

The phone finally chirps my name.

DAZE BECOMES DAYS
THE OTHER SIDE

Dear Donor,

Day 3

I am drifting through breakfast, and I think I am eating. I keep telling myself the episode is merely an obstacle, not a disaster. I do not drink coffee but my insides were churning and I was as jittery as if I had been mainlining java. I am hopeful of some progress and what I could do. I need a quick emotional spackle fix.

Another long wait in ICU. I am a nervous mother hen on a nest of precious eggs. Will that phone ever ring back? Too bad eating fingernails is not nutritious. Finally, passage to the ICU and to Karyn. I hold Karyn's left hand in my left hand and this felt good. I asked her to grip my hand. The fish handshake was weak, but it was there. It was there. Usually my reaction to this kind of handshake is ooh, slimy like a fish. But, it was movement, and helped keep me from losing my grip.

Karyn's eyes ringed with raccoon-like circles of red-purple, IVs and tubes ran from every opening in her body. Nurses shuffled past. Their soft soled shoes, giving an occasional squeak on the well-scrubbed floor.

Karyn needed to concentrate, by looking at her left hand, to move her left arm and hand. Her responses were still one word, but clear. No dialogue. Karyn's short-term memory has been affected. Focus is difficult.

Karyn can move her toes down. No movement in the left leg. Karyn had pain in her chest, soreness around the incision, and coughing hurts.

The doctors and nurses and all the other staff studied Karyn's charts like they were the Dead Sea Scrolls. My mind was tiptoeing through the potential minefields. The doctors were commanders storming the beach at Normandy with wave after wave after wave of soldiers from pulmonology, surgery, thoracic, anesthesiology, vascular, and pharmacy. Soldier ants on a work detail marched quickly back and forth to her cubicle, doing test after test. People and nurses part for the doctors and lung surgeon like Moses at the Red Sea.

The halls are awash with good people seeking answers. The current of doctors goes back and forth to her cubicle. People who truly care for my wife, not as a science experiment, not as a piece of machinery, but as a person. I feel their care and concern, and am warmed like my grandmother's matzah ball soup.

I tell you, this is tough sledding. One of the hardest parts was I wanted to ask Karyn her opinion. What does she think? What should we do? What about an MRI? What about an MRA? What about the trach? What about the GJ feeding tube? I could not ask her the whats. I have been a husband for so long, that when someone asks me, how I am feeling, I turn to Karyn for the answer.

I protected Karyn and Karyn protected me, and I could be stronger than I ever was alone. Time to man up Richard; time to have the strength of two.

A decision was made to trach Karyn, to make it easier to re-vent Karyn if necessary, and to provide suction if needed. The stomach GJ tube will be put in. (I will hear about this—oh, I hope I do, I do) in case there is difficulty in eating and swallowing. Both the trach and GJ tube were not wanted by Karyn, but again, I could not ask her opinion, and I signed off on both. Karyn's condition made both mandatory. The MRA showed signs in the brain that oxygen was not reaching all areas of the brain. The episode was now called "stroke-like" but not a seizure or a stroke.

Day 4—Karyn is using a BiPAP this morning, or rather the BiPAP is using her. The BiPAP takes full control of her breathing. This noisy mask machine inflates the lungs and forces out the carbon dioxide from the system. Her ABG, which checks on the blood gases is strong on oxygen. The doctors want as much of the CO_2 out as possible as LAM places a high amount of this poison in her system—this is why we breathe, to take in the oxygen and force out the carbon dioxide. This morning, Karyn, even with the mask, showed better recognition. Karyn was able to move her left leg over and gave me a soft hand shake with her left hand. Not going to get very many votes with that wet fish.

She looks so good. Finally okay to say it. "You look so good." Her fingertips were pink and her face looked flushed. The highlight of my morning was my wife's glance over to my side of the bed and her hand reaching up and rubbing my shoulder. Love conquers all. Her breathing is so steady and natural that for a moment, I think, it's hard to believe there is anything wrong with her.

Her eyes, so trusting as she looked at me, for some type of reassurance that I would always protect her. I serve as a healing balm and help her stay calm and centered; underneath I was a paddleball, a thin rubber band held me together and I was ready to snap. I am not sure I understood how hard it would really be, like standing at the edge of a cliff, thinking it was just a short drop until I started to fall.

I am using my own BiPAP this morning to force out all those things that are eating away at me, never forgetting how precious the air we share among all of us.

Another long wait in ICU. My sister, Pam, and I just saw Karyn and she was resting comfortably. Karyn was vented last night, so she cannot speak to us. A ventilator breathing tube connected to a machine snaked down inside her, creating a strong smell, antiseptic air, and machines beeped. One machine lets off random unpredictable pings like sonar checking for enemy submarines. Her CO_2 levels remain high. Many different teams, thoracic, pulmonary, hematology, are doing workups as staff hones in on the cause of her episode.

The GJ feeding tube procedure was delayed by radiology as Karyn's blood levels are working so hard, and 2 units will be given this morning. The platelet drop is also being checked. The major anti-rejection drug,

47

Prograf, is being strongly looked at, as the cause of the episode, and a possible replacement, Cyclosporine, is being considered. These are among the primary medicines that trick the body into thinking the new lungs are Karyn's.

The trach is back in play, and there is the strong likelihood that Karyn will be trach'ed which is a short surgical procedure done at bedside so that the venting can be done through the trachea. It will make it easier for Karyn to sit and begin walking. Sitting up and walking are very, very important for your lungs to gain strength. The trach will also make it easier for the bronchostomies to be done. The trach is near the top of Karyn's Hate list. I know from before surgery, the trach (and the GJ tube) are not wanted by her. Not wanted? Hated is a third cousin to the actual word.

Karyn's left side remains weak. She did move her toes and feet up and down this morning. Her left arm remains weak but she was able to move her left hand and arm without looking at them. The best thing today is Karyn is at rest and showing no signs of pain.

It is so very hard to see your loved one, your partner, your best friend, in pain. I hope to God, you, our donor, did not suffer in pain. I wish I could switch places with my wife. I love her more than oxygen. Karyn is my hero for knowing that the other side would be dangerously hard, but never fearing the jump. Here's to better days ahead, and the lifting of the daze.

Day 6—Karyn had a busy day today. Every time I looked out the ICU door, I saw Karyn on the gurney coming and going. The surgeon gave me the option of the trach, the sort of option that really isn't an option at all. Her intubinator was removed, she was trach'd, given two pints of blood, had her platelets checked, had her GJ tube put in, another MRA, and a bronch. The trach brooch is Tiffany silver, not the cheap plastic kind. Maybe one day Karyn will look at the scar on her neck, like it's a tattoo; she can look at it, and say there is a history here, a story to be told.

Pam and I just visited Karyn and she was alert. I can now sense that Karyn is in there. Her eyes no longer haunted; she is watching everything with hawkish intensity. Karyn searches my face like I have the answers to everything. Pam and I showed her photos of the family, and when she was shown pictures of her granddaughter, Avah (who we call Avah Lava), her smile was sooooo big. Maybe we call her Avah Lava because Karyn's mouth exploded like a volcano into a gigantic smile. The nurse was "quizzing" Karyn on what month, who is the President and other questions, and Karyn mouthed all the correct answers.

Karyn now knows she has had a transplant and smiled a smile only second to Avah, when I said she was breathing on room air, and her oxygen level was at 93%. I asked "Karyn Unplugged" for her first dance, and another smile laced her lips. My brain avalanched to my heart.

Pam visited again with one of our fellow lung people—a woman whose husband was also transplanted last weekend. Karyn beamed at seeing her buddy, and I think also felt, that even though she remains in intensive care other people who are not immediate family, can visit. Relief, and more conversation mouthed.

Day 7—Ragged clouds fringed the bluest of skies this morning, and a sweet breeze blew, rustling the leaves in the trees. Visiting Karyn today is like breaking through the clouds and the fog. It was as if the sun came right into our room, clearing the fog from her brain.

Did I tell you her eyes are beautiful? Her lovely peanut butter eyes sparkle brighter with traces of tears of joy. Her eyes scan the room, back and forth, looking for blips on her radar; that another procedure is in the offing.

We have met this morning with the social worker, nurse, chief pulmonologist, and anesthesiologist—their chorus reaffirms our thoughts that Karyn's internal needle has re-centered, and we are enjoying the coming back of the smooth sounds. Karyn's heartbeat, her lung beat, your lung beat, pulsing, remembering, awakening. Donor, I can hear you sigh.

I hate to sound like a Hallmark card, but I just like being with her. She is as comfortable to me as shoes without laces. Sitting and waiting for my next visit, hearing every single tick of the clock. Together, I feel our hearts beat as one. Yesterday, I leaned my cheek against her temple, inhaling her scent as if I could fill myself with it.

Karyn will be weaned off the vent slowly, over the next day or two, and we will meet with all the different therapy teams to work on improving her strength. Pam and I gave her a grease board this morning to write on, and the first missive was, "When will the trach be removed?" Her mouthing went from sleepy to irritation faster than a Ferrari. Vroom. Vroom. Vroom. If her tongue could have come out of her mouth then, she would have been a viper ready to strike. I can smell her fury.

For the trach, I was dressed down like I was a little toddler about to put my fingers in an electrical socket. Karyn's face looked like a kid who did not get what she wanted for Christmas.

Karyn can still not drink water, and her mouth is so dry, like she had wandered in the Sahara Desert for weeks on end.

Each day, I can see the lights being turned back on, one by one. As bright as the sun, my Karyn is back. Letters are being replaced, and the daze is becoming days.

What will it be like when Karyn is no longer tired of being tired? What will it be like to not feel like you are walking through mud? What will it be like to not walk the halls like she's sweeping the floors, a human Swiffer? What will it be like to again take a shower? What will it be like to go for a walk hand-in-hand along with our pooches? What will it be like to take a drink of water and eat solid foods? What will it be like to hold and truly play with Avah? What will it be like?

I can't stop looking at Karyn breathing, her nose naked, without a cannula and tubing. Karyn stares at me so hard that I am afraid I will stop breathing. I realized how much a part of me she is.

This may seem like an insignificant moment, watching Karyn breathe, inhaling through the nostrils, exhaling through the mouth, she feeling the taste and tickle of her own life. But to me this is my world, and Karyn is my universe. You have given Karyn life, and this shall be Karyn's life and Karyn is alive, and she is my life. When I was fourteen or so, my Grandpa Harmon teased me that he would give me a miniature abacus for my birthday. I looked at him puzzled and Grandpa told me, it's the little things that count. You are so right Grandpa. Sometimes the little things are so big. God bless you donor.

Day 8—Karyn had the IV tree removed from the room. The femoral artery plug has been removed. With assistance, she moved from the bed to a reclining chair. Her goal is to sit in the chair for three hours, then move back to the bed. The ventilator will not be used this evening, and if not used for 48 hours, Karyn will step-down from ICU to a regular hospital room. Step-down? Sounds like a step-up. Karyn took six steps to the chair. She is much stronger than the staff thought. Who would have thought the big accomplishment of Karyn's day would be sitting in a chair?

I knew yesterday that Karyn was back both physically and mentally. Her strength, ever-increasing on her left side, and she can move her toes back and forth, effortlessly.

One of the doctors on call walked by her cubicle very early this morning on his rounds, and as he passed, He said "Good Morning" as he walked with a purpose down the ICU hall to another cubicle. Karyn waved back to him with her left arm, smiled, and said "Good morning." The doctor reached the end cubicle, and then walked back and asked Karyn, if she had waved at him. Karyn picked up her left arm, and said, "I guess I did." Later in the day, she could move her left leg.

Mentally, Karyn was back. Pam and I received our marching orders last night. Karyn's sentences spilled, falling over each other, and her words swept across me like a cool breeze. We were told in military-clipped fashion, that we needed to pick up a large fruit basket from the grocery store for the wonderful staff at Duke, a thank-you card, her glasses, magazines, camera, slippers! I sighed so heavily that papers on the nurses' stand across the room wavered. How wonderful to hear her ticking off items. God that felt good. Who knew that receiving barking orders from one's wife could be so heavenly? Her words linger like soft warm air that touches me. The voice was as familiar and as warm as curling up in my bed at night.

Karyn kisses my hand and it sends a spark through me. Her kiss is soft and electric at the same time. Her fingers stroke the inside of my wrists and I burst into flames. Karyn's breath is even now and mine falls in step with her. If anyone had been lost, it was me and I could feel nothing but gratitude at having been found.

My sister knew things were on the way to better times, and left this afternoon for her home. She may be my sis, but she's no sissy.

As evening came, I told Karyn I cannot wait for each morning, to see what progress has been made. In the darkness, I take one of her hands and squeeze it. She squeezes back lightly. I love her hands, they are just the right size. I grabbed that moment and held it close to me, like an amulet, the warmth of her hand. Her eyes are round and brown and fierce and determined. She looked into my eyes, and I looked into hers. I saw so much there. I always would. My eyes would be a hundred years old and still want to keep looking and looking and looking at her.

I told her I so miss being by her side at night, to press our palms together, holding our hands together as one, as we drift off to sleep. Listening to her breathing as she falls asleep, her snoring is a lullaby to me, that she is alive and breathing.

My heart skipped a beat as I floated to the car. The sun is setting and the last pink crayon slashes of light color the sky behind DUKE. The last clinging tendrils of sunlight are slowly disintegrating into the evening sky. Each night as I go to sleep, and right before I fall asleep, I say Good Night Karyn and God Bless You. I say thank you, to you, our donor and May God Bless You. I take a deep breath and exhale a tornado.

I give special thanks to God. Who says that God never gives you more than you can handle? God, we need to talk some more.

Tonight I shall have the deepest, most sound sleep of my life, to sleep without dreams and without ever turning over. My thoughts as I fall asleep are soothing like waves lapping at the shore. I was lost and now I am found.

From the bottom of my lungs,

Richard

INTO THE SECOND WEEK
The Other Side

Dear Donor,

Monday May 25, 2009

Karyn was awakened at 3:30 AM for a bath, a bronch and a walk—aren't there laws against that?

She moseyed about 200 feet in the wee morning hours, then tuckered out, sat in the recliner by her bed for three hours. Two more chest tubes removed and two drains to go.

By tomorrow morning, Karyn will be off the dreaded vent for more than 48 hours and step-down may happen at that time. Accent on the "may happen."

In the afternoon, I was sitting in the ICU waiting room, decorated (and that is generous) like early Motel 6, but would look much better with the lights off. Just outside the door, stood Karyn, holding the two handles of the high boy Swedish walker. She invited me to join the caravan, and off we went, doing a circle of the ICU outside hallways, walking over 350 feet! Blood pressure was low, but not scary low, and no dizziness. Karyn was spent from her work-out, but full of smiles, spending the rest of the day in bed grabbing some much-needed sleep.

Tuesday, May 26, 2009

Karyn's CO2 levels rose to 65 last night, and she had to be re-vented from 1:00 AM to 6:00 AM. She sat in the chair for the full five hours. Blood pressure remains low. Karyn went for a walk with the high boy walker, and reached 350 feet. I had the important job in the entourage; walking behind with a chair, in case she needed to sit down. (To leave the hospital from step-down, you must walk 5280 feet, a mile).

Karyn may take a swallow test tomorrow, to see if she can eat regular food (Is hospital food regular?) She may also require an MRI later today.

Wednesday May 27th

The sky outside Karyn's hospital room is griddled gray and orange, and a light wind moves through the trees outside the ICU window, so that the trees seem to dance. She is resting now after her 10:00 AM 800 foot walk. 3 laps and exhaustion takes her into sleep. Last night the evil CO2 levels again rose dangerously to 65, and Karyn was re-vented for 4 hours. The vent makes sleep hard, alarms going off, and breathing for her at a different pace, contracting harder against her stomach.

Maybe one day soon, she will wake up feeling gooder as one Southern gentleman spoke of in the ICU waiting room this morning. An easy day, is like turning on the lights, one by one.

No complaints from Karyn, other than if they try to re-vent her tonight, she'll run away.

Thursday May 28th

Last night, while cramped in the ICU waiting room, longing for the space of a Southwest Airline seat, I looked up and Karyn was outside the door, ready to go for a walk. I joined the parade with her two attendants, and we walked for almost ten feet, when a chest tube came out. Out. O. U. T. That shouldn't happen. The parade marched back to ICU, without me in tow, and I was back in the economy section waiting an hour and a half to again see Karyn. Surgery had been set for later that night to reattach the tube.

Going back home last night wondering whether Karyn would be vented for the evening, Wondering how Karyn would be in the morning.

Early Friday morning the 29th, the sky was a brilliant blue and endless. Why does everything have a different slant to it in the morning? Mornings are hopeful. Nights, especially the deepest part of the night after I awake suddenly, seem to intensify troubles and worries. Everything small become large, everything bad becomes worse

This morning, in the shower lathering up and watching bubbles rise from my hands, one bobbles as it floats upwards. I imagined it growing larger and larger filling up the shower until Glinda the Good Witch of the North would come forth from the filmy shell in a quick pop to grant my every wish. To make everything perfect. Perfect lungs, perfect Karyn. Perfect.

Rushing to get dressed and I can't wait to get into ICU at 9, the good witching hour, when visiting hours start. Karyn looks great this morning. No vent last night, even though her CO2 level climbed to 60, but finally the staff agreed, to use the "look test"—if she looked good, leave her be. Her bicarbonate level in her blood and the alkalinity of her blood is compensating for the higher CO2 level. No vent, did you hear that? No vent—let me vent my feelings. Thank you Glinda acting on behalf of God.

I want smooth even roads without bumps, but I guess God just likes to go off-roading

Karyn walked 1200 feet this morning. I listened so closely to her breathing that I began breathing in the same rhythm. In, fill your lungs completely and hold it. Exhale entirely and push out every drop of air with your diaphragm. A few stops—no pain while walking—no alarms going off on the blood pressure meter as her BP stays up

Rumor has it Karyn will step down either later this evening or tomorrow and no, I did not start the rumor

Mornings do look better.

Friday May 29th

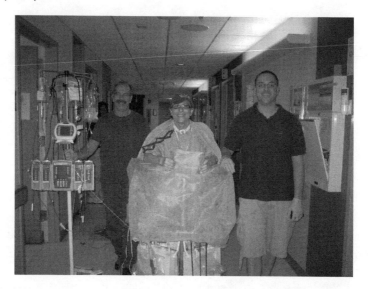

Step down day—room 3316! Karyn has been moved to a regular room. T 3000 wing has the tiniest hospital rooms ever. How I long for the wide open spaces of the ICU waiting room. The noise and activity level on the wing are greatly reduced from the ICU. Tomorrow I will decorate her room with posters I made pre-transplant. Posters of photos of the family and our dogs, which are family. We will make the—little-room-that-could homey.

Karyn has a weariness in her voice and lines beneath her eyes and nose that stretch to her ears seem sharper and deeper. Her eyes bounce around like popcorn, seeing everything in the hall and in her room, all at one time.

Sitting in my chair by the bed for minutes at a time I felt removed from it all as though I was watching it from afar, and envying the man sitting with the woman. My breath coming out in steady streams like car exhaust

Days in which time has been measured in a haphazard fashion; days in which unreal and unpredictable things have become common. Yesterday a new chest tube placed into Karyn, where one had fallen out. How does a chest tube fall out? X rays showed the new tube needed to be moved—twice—chest tube moves, x rays, repositioning—new catheter tube placed in upper right lung where there is a small pneumo-thorax. But as Karyn says, "Hey 98% of my lungs work fine." A far cry from both lungs, equaling 8% pre-transplant. As we prepare for the last and third walk of the day, instead an X Ray.

Karyn now asleep and when she wakes we will walk—a promise of 5 laps. Karyn walked 4 laps (1200 feet) this morning. To move to the third step, out of the hospital and the 23 days of rehab at the Center for Living, she must walk 20 laps in a day and have all the tubes removed. Luckily on the 13th day, I don't have to light a fire under Karyn. Her home fires burn within.

Looking forward to the walks; I so love the walks. When I was kid, I had to walk five miles through the snow, just to change the channel for my parents, but then I was the neighbor kid's imaginary friend. Humor lets me know things are getting much better.

Looking forward to the days passing, as they should, like the turning of pages in a quiet, lovely book.

Sunday May 31st

One giant leap

Karyn has made great strides since Friday. Walking into her room seeing her sleeping peacefully on the bed, and not seeing her gasp for air, was the first sign something was different. When she awoke, I took her for a walk without oxygen, and at lap 3 she turned to tell me to keep up with the entourage of IV tubes, not realizing that she can now talk while walking. Yes, she can walk and talk at the same time. Chewing gum will come later.

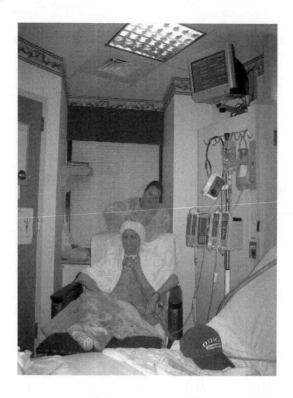

Yesterday, Saturday, she walked twelve laps around the triangle corridor. The doctor in the morning was impressed as twelve was the goal for the entire day. Today, Sunday was an amazing day even with the pneumothorax and we got up to walk for the second time around 11 AM. The mornings are always a little more trying and Karyn feels a bit more stiff and needed two or three breaks during the walk. After the first walk, the new arrivals, my son and daughter-in-law pampered Karyn by shaving her legs and giving her a beautiful pedicure, an awesome hot pink, followed by massaging her legs with a stress relieving lotion. Karyn finished a total of 18 laps around the unit which equals one mile. It wasn't easy but as we rounded each corner staff and other patients and their families cheered us on. One of her nurses noted that he has two other patients, neither of whom had as invasive a surgery and yet Karyn was walking more laps. Now if we can get rid of the many tubes and IV cords that are attached

One more x ray today, another tomorrow and hopefully your lungs will show progress forward.

Karyn walking one mile; was like watching Kirk Gibson clobber the world series home run. Walking one mile made for a grand slam day.

Talk to you soon, our donor.

Richard

THE OTHER SIDE

Dear Donor,

Monday June 1, 2009

Karyn had an early walk this morning, and surprised PT with seven laps—the expectation was six. The doctor came by and said another chest x-ray was needed and probably another chest tube would be removed. The upper right hand portion of the right lung will not inflate. The chest tube brings suction to assist the lung in fully expanding. The tube is put in without any meds and shall I say it hurts. How many tubes can one person have in their chest area?

Looking forward to meeting with the pharmacy pulmonologist today, who will advise us on the drug protocol after we leave the hospital. This meeting is very positive, as the hospital only does this as you near the end of your stay. There are many drugs on the list so by the time you finish, you start over with the first one: It sure seems that way.

We walked three laps later in the morning and Karyn was dizzy. Her pulse ox showed 100! I do not know if she was just plumb tuckered out but I put her to bed. Then the vampire phlebotomist came and I sent her away, telling her to come back tomorrow for the ABG. (I will hear about this). Then respiratory therapy came by later, and did their tests. How apropos that one of the tests has Karyn sticking her tongue out. The Pulmonary Function test was the best ever, even with the pneumo. Then another chest x-ray.

Karyn went back to sleep and when a doctor came in, she woke up out of her stupor and saw her transplant surgeon. She knew immediately what this meant: another chest tube, and God Bless Her, she did not stick her tongue out. The half hour procedure took an hour and a half, but it is believed the air came out of the lung, and the right lung pushed back into its original shape prior to the pneumo caused by the chest tube falling out. Another chest x-ray was being done on our pooped-out girl as I left for the evening. Hopefully the lung is back, the scary part is that if not, the lung can fill with liquid and turn to solid.

Tuesday June 2nd

Extra! Extra? Read All About It: Princess Readies Leave from Duke

We met with post-transplant coordinator with a full meeting late tomorrow morning. The lung is fully expanded and there are no leaks. Hopefully by the end of this week, Karyn will leave the hospital. "End of Week" in hospital talk means Friday or maybe the weekend or maybe Monday.

I am learning how to give insulin shots (some transplant patients are diabetic, either short-term or for the rest of their lives). I have given Karyn four of her last shots, and she is still talking to me. I will be graded on shot-giving later today.

I have also learned how to use the GJ tube for medications and feedings. Karyn passed the second part of her swallow test. What a smile on her face as she got to drink a little bit of water with one of her medications this morning. Ah, the smell of that bouquet: tap water 2009, a great vintage. Karyn cannot drink water by itself, and must take her pills with chin down to separate the trachea from the esophagus, to lessen the danger of aspirating into her lungs. A treadmill has been placed in her room, as there are not enough Swedish high boy walkers available. Her exercise goes on though she is complaining about how slow the treadmill moves. She would rather be walking the halls. But this is easier for me, as moving four suction machines to a walker is quite a feat.

Wednesday June 3rd

I had hoped to find many tubes removed this morning, but only one had been taken out before I arrived. The concern is to make sure the right lung stays fully inflated. I helped Karyn onto the treadmill and although she walked very slowly, she did the full 20 minute regimen, which seemed like it took an hour. How she hated the very slow setting of the treadmill. She's still in a lot of pain as she is healing quite fast, which makes her chest all-the-more tighter. The med cocktails are making her tired and woozy.

As I was walking the halls of third floor today, a young girl of maybe 8 or 9 came out of a room, approached me, and asked, "What's wrong with that lady you were walking with yesterday?" I explained that the lady, my wife, recently had a double lung transplant, and was given two new lungs. I was pretty darn impressed that this little girl asked about my wife, that she obviously was clearly used to speaking to grown-ups. But then, she turned back into a little kid. "My great-grandma's 95. Will your wife live to be 95?" Will she live as long as my Grandma Ethel? She had asked this with a little bit more urgency, with the concern that children can show in a way that breaks your heart. I immediately ran through answers, and after a brief hesitation, quickly said matter of factly, "Yes, she will live to 95."

I have no qualms about answering that way. I don't think any good would have come from the unvarnished truth. What else was I going to say? I wasn't going to explain the average life expectancy of a double lung transplant is around 10 years, that at 5 years out, 50 out of 100 are no longer with us, dying of viruses like cytomegalovirus (CMV) or of BOS rejection. There will be plenty of time for that sweet little girl to hear about life, to learn that it contains sorrows as well as joys, to hear that bad things do happen to good people. All that lies ahead of her, Donor, I wasn't going to be that person, to start that part of life earlier. Life will take care of that.

For that moment at least, she was pretty sure that all was right in the world, and those moments are pretty darn precious in anyone's life. And Donor, who is to say, how many years Karyn will have?

Watching that little girl skipping down the hall, I am taking it day by day.

Thursday June 4th

Another stage looms. Sometime tomorrow, Karyn will be released from the hospital. One tube remains. The two catheter drainage bulbs will be taken out tomorrow. A new metal trach has been fastened around Karyn's neck. A lovely smaller choker from Tiffany's. (DUKE, you shouldn't have). I passed the trach-cleaning test. Talk about gooey yuck in the throat. The last of the chest tubes was pulled this afternoon. Karyn down to x-ray to make sure your lungs are all in order. This morning her O2 was 100! A perfect score. Karyn is acing her tests at DUKE. We have walked almost a mile of halls today and will do more in a little while. Karyn worked with the speech therapist, who is also the swallow therapist. She had more swallows than Capistrano and, hopefully, doctor's orders will be up-dated to allow soft foods by mouth, which would include thickened liquids. Being released on Friday is perfect as it will give us two days to set up the regimen at home at the Residence Inn and then start the mandatory 23 days of rehab at the Center for Living. Karyn will handle the 23 days like our Golden, Bo, handles a bone. Bo grabs it, grips it, looks around dreamily while chomping at it, and won't let anyone take it away from him. Karyn can taste the bone, and I can see the sun setting over the Rocky Mountains this evening.

Thanks for being with me Donor,

Richard

DUKE AND EVALUATIONS
THIS SIDE

Dear Diary,

We were active for a double lung transplant at University Hospital in Denver for 30 months. Not one call. The clock was ticking; its sound louder and louder. *I could really die. What if I never got lungs?*

Karyn and I evaluated other hospitals in the United States, checking their protocols and UNOS statistics. We considered some very fine hospitals, including Cleveland Clinic, University of Pittsburgh, Barnes Jewish, Stanford, UCLA and DUKE. We chose DUKE for its excellent rehabilitation program, its high number of lung transplants, its propensity to do double lung transplants rather than single lung transplants, and its very quick wait time to transplant once listed.

In March of 2009, we ran the evaluations gauntlet at DUKE Medical Center. I can still see Karyn, slumped over in her wheel chair, going from test to test to test. So exhausted. Her body shrinking into itself. Sucking air, like a fish out of water. From our hikes in Zion, to our dog walks in the neighborhood, to only being able to be driven someplace to eat. Now in a wheelchair to get from place to place. Her shrunken life now was eating, sitting, and sleeping.

Monday morning was an orientation meeting, and then on to clinic to have 25 vials of blood taken. Afterwards, we met with the social worker, nutritionist, and back to clinic to leave more bodily fluids, this of the yellow variety. Back in the wheel chair to be raced off for chest x-rays, and a differential VQ scan. The last test was in nuclear medicine, where a technician held a mask around Karyn's mouth and nose for five minutes. *Are they trying to smother me? I try hard to forget that the tech is releasing a radioactive gas for me to breathe in. Then they give me an injection of a radioactive isotope and more scans over 45 minutes. Tonight my husband can read by my night light.*

Tuesday morning we head down the road from DUKE Medical Center to the Center for Living. The CFL is the pulmonary rehabilitation location. A physical therapist takes down all of Karyn's information and tests her for muscle strength. There is a short exercise pep talk from the PT. You must walk 1000 feet in 6 minutes. Karyn's heart and blood pressure are checked both before and after the walk. You must walk at least 1000 feet in 6 minutes or you will not be accepted into the transplant program. You must show heart to get into the lung program. Karyn cranked up her oxygen and made the 1000 feet with a few seconds to spare.

Then back to DUKE Medical Center for the esophageal manometry and a 24 hour pH probe. A tech sprayed Karyn's throat with Lidocaine until it felt difficult to swallow. The technician next put a Lidocaine swab up Karyn's nose to deaden it, and then inserted a small tube, which goes up the nose and into the stomach. *Can you say gag?*

Over the next half hour, the tech squirts a bit of saline into my mouth and asks me to swallow once. If I double swallow before I get another squirt, it does not count towards the 10 swallows needed. Each time I swallowed, my throat became sorer. Let's just say it was miserable. Once they pulled the catheter out, I had a few minutes to regroup and then the process started all over again. More Lidocaine. This time, the catheter inserted into my nose and threaded down into my stomach is much smaller. The probe is hooked into a monitor I wear about my neck. I must record every time I eat or drink anything and when I stop. The monitor can show a correlation between what I eat and when excess stomach acid begins. The tech looked me in the eye and staring at me, said, "I only ask two things. Don't hit me and don't vomit in my face." No fist fights broke out and there was no projectile vomiting. The probe is kind of clever in a sadistic kind of way. I now have the probe in and am able to eat with minimal discomfort. Results will indicate whether there is acid reflux and a probable need for a Nissen Fundiplication stomach wrap surgery after transplant.

Wednesday morning could not come fast enough as far as my throat was concerned. I arrived at the hospital early so the probe could be removed. On to the liver ultrasound. I relaxed on the table while ultrasound jelly was smeared around my lower right ribs and belly. Next onto to radiology for a fluoroscopy of my diaphragm. The machine took pictures while I perform different types of breaths in different positions.

Now the fun ends with a barium swallow study. In high school I memorized the periodic table of elements. Just because they can be consumed does not mean they are appetizing. The drink is almost more solid than liquid. You could use the cup for a dumbbell. The barium inflates my stomach and I need to roll around to give the camera many views.

On Thursday, I have an echocardiogram. Then the heart catherization. The numbing and threading parts are not too comfortable. I cough and am asked not to cough. I cough again. Easy for them to say, hard for me to do.

On the fifth day, we scurry to get in all the tests and meetings. Pulmonary function test in the morning. Arterial blood gas draw. Then to meet the financial coordinator. Luckily, we have strong insurance, and this is not a financial roadblock. How sad when someone cannot be transplanted because of lack of insurance or lack of funds. CT scan of sinuses and my lungs. With contrast. I feel flushed and like I need to pee or maybe like I did. Another IV and dye. Richard and his sister went in the afternoon in search of places to stay. DUKE has an excellent satellite system of housing, and Richard picked the Residence Inn in Durham. There is a good-sized group of lung patients there, and it will be good to be around others, sharing a common experience. It's a real plus, to be among your own kind, all going through the same program.

We left for home, and the wait for the call. Will I get in? Monday was the beginning of the waiting game. The transplant committee meets on Tuesday mornings and you are notified Thursday or Friday. You must then relocate to DUKE as soon as possible.

COMING TO DUKE
THIS SIDE

Dear Diary,

DUKE just called and said, "Come as soon as possible." I am breathless even sitting with my oxygen turned up. We leave this Sunday, March 22nd, for the 1800 mile drive through nine states to my destiny. We will arrive on Tuesday and make our home at the Residence Inn in Durham. We will take the first 5 days to settle in, put some food in the cupboards, and of course find someone to do my hair.

I start working out next week at the DUKE Center For Living. It's required. One of the reasons I chose DUKE is they want me healthy and strong. Can a person who is awaiting a double lung transplant be healthy and strong? Well, they want me as healthy and as strong as I can be. That means a minimum of twenty three sessions at the Center for Living, which will take anywhere from five to six weeks, working out four hours a day, Monday through Friday, and attending the Center's transplant school.

The greatest part of all that, a week or so after completing the required sessions, DUKE activates you for transplant, and the average wait time for lungs is 19 days. Air, here I come. A taste sweeter than any fine wine.

It all seems unreal and I wonder what awaits me on the other side,

Karyn

Richard Schad

Saturday

Dear Diary,

It's spring here. Spring is wonderful, makes you feel like . . . blowing your nose and wiping your eyes. Rich, I need my Claritin!

When we arrived here I was feeling very sick and tired. I do not even remember the drive. Rich drove the entire way, and I slept almost the entire way. When I started rehab at the CFL, I could barely work out and was a real whiner. Turning away from my difficulties and fears has helped me move forward all these years. I now know I must deal with my fears to move ahead and into recovery after surgery.

Moving forward,

Karyn

Sunday

Dear Diary,

Many ups and downs this week. Last Wednesday, I had an incredible work-out. I walked more laps in 20 minutes than I ever did in 30 minutes. Yippee!

The next day was not so good. I woke up and had trouble breathing. We had to meet with a psychologist because they thought I needed coping with panic. I had stopped taking Xanax when DUKE had called and said to come on down but only after I had weaned off of it. THEY thought I would not push through after surgery because of my panic. DO THEY KNOW ME!?

Nothing will stop me,

Karyn

Sunday

Dear Diary,

Going through so much anxiety and anger at not being listed, and this week had been incredibly hard breathing. When my breathing gets hard, I question if my disease has worsened, or is it allergies or am I merely sick? So two days ago the answer came. I am sick and need antibiotics. I am doing much better today and Rich and I walked the nearby mall. Hopefully soon, I will be listed.

Getting my breath (if I can call it that) back,

Karyn

Tuesday

Dear Diary,

I AM LISTED! I AM LISTED! Can you see my smile in writing that sentence? The average wait time for lungs is 19 days. Yes, I know that is an average. So let us hope that God finds the right lungs for me very soon. Let's also pray for the Donor and the Donor's family, who will make this incredible decision as they save a life and lose their loved one.

Bye for now,

Karyn

We Are All In This Together and We Are Here To Do Our Best
Both Sides

DUKE requires 23 full days of rehab in order to be listed and DUKE also requires 23 full days post-transplant of rehab, at the Center for Living.

Before transplant, Karyn suffered from shortness of breath, and increased oxygen needs. Her activity level, if I can call it that, had decreased to almost nothing. Her respiratory, postural, trunk, arm, and leg muscles had wasted away. There was fear and anxiety due to breathlessness. There was cardiovascular lack of condition.

The lung transplant improves shortness of breath and oxygen need, but only a comprehensive rehabilitation program can improve the other issues. There just is no substitute for exercise and activity.

Rehabilitation not only improves cardiopulmonary function and quality of life, but also counteracts some of the side effects of medication. The lungs are the body's oxygenator and what exercise does is train your muscles to use the oxygen that is available most efficiently.

The Center for Living rehabilitation program strengthened her body in preparation for specific tasks and activities. Before transplant, the simple act had become not so simple. Just picking up something from the floor was a challenge because bending had been compromised by the over-crowded conditions in her chest caused by the expansion of her diseased lungs. End-stage lung disease made the easiest of tasks seem like the stairs to the top of the Statue of Liberty.

The Center provided a specialized and personalized exercise program which prepared Karyn for her surgery and recovery. The sessions were every Monday through Friday, from 12:30 to 3:30, and several times each week at transplant school for an hour lecture after work-outs.

Getting the most out of the least prepared Karyn for the transplant and, I truly believe, saved her life after the "stroke-like episode."

May 4, 2009

Dear Diary,

I feel myself winning back my body. The workouts at the CFL may not be the workouts you see on the Biggest Loser, but I and all the others at the Center are all winners.

I trudge up the hill to the Center each day. Just opening the heavy door takes so much of my strength. Sometimes, I just wait for someone to come outside. God, thank you, someone is leaving and opening the door for me. I feel like I am suffocating and cannot take another step. I check in and shamble over to the milk crates on the table, pulling out my clipboard and pencil. I swap out my oxygen tank for the Big "E" green monster cylinder critter. I use a walker/

seat combination for stabilization and for my oxygen anchor. One day on the other side I will talk and not push my tank burden in front of me.

One of the trainers goes over questions with me, checking my blood pressure, O2 level, pain number, and weight. Even though all of us at the CFL have a lung disease, we are all different. Each disease is different and even people with the same disease are at different places. No two people experience the same thing or are on the same level. I try my darndest not to compare myself to others and what they can do. (But I do anyway).

After the trainer finishes his or her questions, I shuffle over to the center gym floor. I lie on the mat and do arm and leg raises. I strap on leg weights, which weigh from 1to 3 pounds. These weights and the therapy bands provide resistance during leg lifts and ankle rotations. I use dumb bells to increase my arm strength. The trainer guides me through a solid non-stop forty-five minute workout.

The trainers rotate and teach different regimens. Each of the trainers is very helpful. They are knowledgeable and determined to help me have a successful operation and recovery. No pain, no gain. I must be making huge gains. The trainers watch us, watching without hovering, helping with equipment, giving me lots of smiles and encouragement. Courage is wrapped in Encouragement.

We are taught breathing guidance, diaphragmatic breathing. Breathe in through your nose for 2 counts and exhale for 4 counts through pursed lips. I place my hand just below my rib cage and past my belly button. I make my hand rise when I inhale deeply through my nose and then drop it, when I exhale through those pursed lips. Mouth breathers use auxiliary muscles in the neck and shoulders and invite shallow breathing, which can lead to shortness of breath.

It feels like I work one solid hour. We turn our heads left and right, up and down, raise our trembling arms and legs, and march while lying on our back with our feet up in the air, raising our butts.

After floor exercises and stretching our muscles we get a short break, and the snack in my lunch box is waiting.

Then walking, weights and the bike.

We pre-transplant people are easy to spot. When we walk, we are just so busy concentrating on walking, there is little or no talk. Just trying to breathe is hard work, and we do not have the breath to chat with those sitting or walking next to us. The post-transplant people, do they EVER stop talking? I wonder how many words I have saved up, when I will be unencumbered by shortness of breath?

All of us at CFL are each other's biggest fans and supporters. I don't think I ever walked a lap without seeing a smiling face. I also save up some of my breath to encourage others. It takes just a moment of time, but I know it can provide all the difference for someone struggling. As Richard's grandma always said, we all got here on a different ship, but we are all in the same boat.

I save the rest of my talking for when break time comes, for the before and the after, when my O2 comes back to earth.

After the short break, we are rotated to a different station. Weights today, bikes tomorrow, and reverse.

I have my lap counting rope, a cord of about 30 little plastic colored beads. Trainers set a timer for a 20 minute walk, except on Tuesday and Thursday and then, ugh, we have to walk 30 minutes. We sound like a steam engine, with our oxygen pumping. Each time I walk a lap, I move a bead. I feel like my body is getting that second wind. My eyes itch and my airways close up—who has violated the no perfume rule in the CFL? Certain synthetic chemicals compromise lungs and airways. I gasp for more oxygen. My throat swells and I have an uncontrolled coughing attack.

I move onto the weights. On alternate days, I work upper body and lower body. Physical therapy has evaluated my ability, and developed a weight plan for me to gradually build my strength up. There are four or five different machines for the upper body and other challenges such as lifting hand weights and squats. I stretch my muscles in my legs. I look around and notice that no two plans are alike. The workout is a process, a balance for my condition. The process, always changing, to get the most out of me, so I will be at my strongest when I have the surgery.

Next comes the bikes, which are actually called Nu-Step. I am seated in a recumbent position, just like sitting in a car. My feet are extended onto foot pads. Instead of rotating my feet in a circular motion like on a bicycle, I use stepping motions to apply pressure on the steps. The bike measures my distance, level of resistance, watts produced, and steps taken. Some people, I see, use the two handles to strengthen their arms and assist with the force requirements. Want me to use my feet only? Look ma, no hands. No hands to help supply some of the energy needed for rotations. My legs do all the work. What level am I on? For sure, the level will be increased tomorrow or the next day by the ever-watchful trainer.

Once or twice a week, after the workouts, there is an hour lecture. Transplant School shows us the many different phases of what we will see, hear, feel, encounter, as well as some of the more difficult subjects to bear, like what could go wrong, tubes stuck in our bellies, diabetes and shots, speech therapy, caregivers support, medicines and pills, stomach wrap, and the list continues. I soak up all the information. The more Richard and I know, the more we won't be scared or startled when a nurse or doctor tells us what is next.

I swap out my oxygen tanks, throw my dirty towels in the bin, gather up my lunchbox, and make my way outside through the heavy door to my awaiting carriage for the ride home, and much-needed sleep. The door feels a little lighter. I am the biggest winner.

Can't keep my eyes open,

Karyn.

June 5, 2009

On The Other Side

Der Tag

The morning we leave the hospital, Karyn idles in a chair several feet from the IV pole adjacent to her bed. There is a service tag dangling from the side of the pole. Karyn blows out air aimed directly at the tag, and the tag shakes.

A wild-west shoot-out, with Karyn's breath her six gun, and the bad guy, the tag, falls back. A little kid's giggles cross her face, and she covers her mouth. Karyn is again four years old, and just blew out all the candles on her cake. What a big girl I am. Her present to both of us is being able to blow out. Before transplant, Karyn could not blow out a single candle, even if the candle was right in front of her mouth. Her own life was on a short wick.

The sparkle has returned to her eyes, her eyes dancing around the room. I reveled in this moment watching my wife breathe, seeing the healthy color of her skin, hearing the sound of her breath in and out, tasting her air, and listening to her lungs purr like a well-loved kitten.

Pure delight washes across her face. Her brown eyes were holding mine. I could hear the grin in her voice. "Watch this." "Look at me." "Look at what I can do." "Watch!" Karyn flashes me a smile, a smile brighter than an amusement park at night. More giggles. Her words curl around my heart and my mind dances a jig. Her laughter tinkles like chimes in the wind. I could see an imprint of every pleasing smile that had ever stretched across her lips in that deep laugh. I laughed with her, but mostly

I wanted to watch her laugh, and a small part of me wanted to be Karyn at that moment.

Her smile is so warm, chocolate is melting in the vending machines down the hall. The most exquisite smile I have ever seen; I felt a shot of love so powerful it hurt my chest. Warmth crept up my body, landed somewhere near its center. A thousand suns rise from my chest. Karyn is breathing life in.

She flashes me the most adorable grin ever. I exult in the moment and my breath comes out like it had been trapped.

When Karyn took a break from blowing at the tag, I felt like we were the only two people in the world. I love you Karyn, more than I can tell you, more than I even realized until I understood I could lose you. I felt my heart swell with tenderness and love and an awesome thankfulness to the God who not only heard my prayers but also answered them. When you love someone, you can see all their mess and their brokenness, and you love them anyway. Just maybe, maybe, it makes you love them even more. I felt the truth as deeply as anything I have ever felt, and I could barely breathe.

Karyn blows at the tag over and over and over, "Hey, look at this, look what I can do." The poor tag unfurls the white flag. Karyn again, "Watch me, watch this." She giggles another smile that transforms her face and it seems somehow spotlighted from a heavenly light. Her smile is like a ray of sunlight, the kind that pierces clouds at an angle and makes you think about heaven.

I am buzzing from her smile, and being so close to her I feel light-headed and invincible, drunk on love. Can air be addictive? Even the paint is being charmed off the wall. I leaned my cheek against her temple, inhaling her scent as if I could fill myself with it.

Karyn is breathing air right in front of my face, exulting in her new lungs and the sheer joy of breathing. This is a miracle.

The air she is breathing, I am breathing. We are breathing it together, breathing life in. Thank you donor. I feel like I am sitting in the sunshine on a cold day, and I feel warmth coming from the barking of her laughter. She leans in so that her head is close to mine. I can taste her breath when she talks. Her words flow as naturally as her breath. Her eyes light up again and again, and her cheeks crinkle. Karyn is happier than a bird with a French fry.

Ah, this is one of those moments in life, when you know you are having one of those moments in life. My cheeks are wet and I do not even remembering starting to cry. Karyn is peeling back all the years, and I see the young girl at camp with lips of white-pink neon gloss. I felt the planet stop rotating for just the tiniest fraction of a second to pay tribute.

I take a deep breath in, a deep clear breath, and I hold it. I let it out. I do it again and again and again and again, the way one plays their favorite song, that they just cannot get enough of. Never gets old, the feeling, the rush of fresh oxygen spilling into my lungs and into my heart, racing through my blood vessels to feed me the life that I once so longed for. Each breath my system craves. Each exhalation my body rejoices. My heart and lungs, my body and soul, feel like new lovers that cannot get enough of one another.

A nurse watching Karyn blow at the tag, had never heard of LAM. She had read up on it, reading the information on the LAM Foundations' website, thelamfoundation.org, and asked many questions about the disease. When Karyn explained just how rare the disease is, the nurse commented, "You must feel really unlucky." Karyn replied, "No, I actually feel lucky—through LAM, I have met so many Lammies who are my sisters—I am the lucky one." Karyn does make me feel like she's the lucky one. LAM and lung disease are definitely not a gift, but to see the good through the bad, this is a gift.

We walked the halls of step-down one last time. Karyn leaned, entwined in my arm, as her balance was a little unsteady. As we walked out the door of her room to the long hall, my arms roped around her waist, I felt as-if we were newly married and heard in my head, a voice that proclaimed ladies and gentlemen, for the first time anywhere, I present to you, Mr.

and Mrs. Richard Schad. I present to you Karyn Schad, who takes my breath away.

The universe hangs on a kiss, exists in the hold of a kiss. Richard, you may now kiss the bride. A kiss I could relive again and again, stored away in my memory like a DVD I can call up anytime, pause, rewind, fast forward and then slow motion to that kiss.

I could feel people's eyes on me, feel them watching our every move, and not in a bad way, like they were making fun of me or something, but like I was Cinderella walking up the steps in a fairy tale with a prince.

The rest of the day blurs together. We are inundated by staff, one person after another after another after another came to sign off our leaving the hospital. Doctors and staff and pharmacists and psychologists, bumping into each other, "Oh I'll just come back." The stream of people turned into a flood. The psychologist came to check on us, the pharmacist came with prescriptions and changes in medications, the diabetic nurse came to check on us and make sure I knew how to give the shots, the oxygen company who also provides cleaning supplies for the trach came to show me how to clean the trach and to re-vent Karyn if necessary, and another person came to show how to set-up and use the IV tower for GJ tube feedings, and clean it. Phew! "Did I say, phew!"

Finally, the pulmonologist came and removed the last two drainage bulbs from Karyn and she was unchained.

The life game of Tag, You're It. Ollie, Ollie Oxygen Free.

Leaving Hospital,
Friday June 5ᵗʰ – Tag You're It
The Other Side

Dear Donor,

For the first time, I stepped outside the hospital after my double lung transplant. It was late afternoon, a beautiful late spring day, but beautiful is inadequate. The electricity in the air had changed, and I could smell the ions dancing. The colors that day were turned up, as if I had been seeing with blurred vision before. The scents in the air were almost over-powering—growing flowers, traffic rush, food smells. Even the time of day; late afternoon smells different from early morning or evening. I felt I had hit a pause button on life.

Everything was more three-dimensional, more alive than anything seen under the flat fluorescent indoor lighting of the hospital. I felt like I had been wearing ear plugs and they had fallen out and everything that was muffled is now so clear and vibrant. The sounds rushed at me. Voices, no longer filtered or muffled by hospital walls, had a different ring outside. I heard a dog bark, a horn honk, a child yell, shoes hitting pavement and multiple conversations going on around me. Even walking felt different than it had in hospital hallways.

There was a light breeze and I could feel my skin. My fingertips were pink and not gun-metal gray and my face felt flushed. My face had gone from tombstone gray to a serious scarlet. How wonderful the breeze smelled—it smelled like sunshine—like sunshine and freshly-mowed grass. I could not stop breathing it, filling my lungs again and again with the sweetest smell I'd ever tasted. The sky was the color of blue porcelain, and the air had texture, as it touched my face, my arms, and my new lungs. After ten years on supplemental oxygen, I can breathe on my own. The sun, it warmed me from the outside in. I felt like a flower blossoming in the spring, coming back to life. I turned my face to the sun and the shadows fell behind me.

Had the world always been like this, this alive? I vowed never to forget this moment. I could feel every joy and sorrow and goodness and sadness and sweetness and beauty and hope and past and present and every perfect thing. Silence might allow this moment to last forever, which would still not be enough. It was like God had flipped on the switch of the world and everything is just now on. The "episode" gave ground and a million switches were turned on, my motherboard energized and euphoric. I know that such delicious intensity can not last, but I will remember. I will remember what it was like to be reborn. I took a deep breath, a pain-free breath of fresh air. Had air ever tasted this good? I looked back at DUKE Medical Center, and up to the sky. In the space between was my whole life.

I am afraid that such delicious intensity cannot last, but I shall remember. I shall always remember what it was like to be reborn.

Donor, we have become each other's air,

Karyn

Dear Donor,

When the soft swish of the automatic door at Duke closed, I knew another door was opening. A breeze washed over us, like the hands of you, our donor, caressing us. The air felt so good, so soft and comfortable. Karyn and I stared at each other for long moments, and in those moments, all of our time together and to be passed between us. A memory I wanted to keep whole and recall again and again. God, if that wonderful rush of the senses could be bottled, it would be worth a thousand times its weight in gold.

I stared at Karyn and could not stop smiling; her smiles felt like sun on my face. The sun made her look tinged with gold, as if she was lit up from the inside. This girl was drunk on 100 per cent proof air. There is red through her cheeks, like mercury rising in an early summer thermometer over the

North Carolina triangle. The gratitude she feels to you and DUKE is indescribable. A sigh of relief, one deep breath, says it all. I am standing very close to her, and my head is buzzing, like those many years ago when she had written her phone number on my binder cover.

Karyn is on full blast and I along with everyone else am on mute. Seeing her in daylight is like switching the channel to high-definition. Karyn is tasting the sweetness of the spring air, and gulping it into her living, breathing heart-beating body of hers. Just like her playfulness with the IV tag, everything was new to her, which made it new for me. I feel like a teenager, flushed and eager for my first date. Can I click a magical stopwatch and exist in this moment forever? A butterfly alights nearby, and inside my heart I feel the lightest flutter in my chest, delicate little butterfly wings beating in sync with my own heartbeat. Now when I see butterflies I shall smile. Maybe this is what Karyn saw in the hospital.

Donor, Karyn does nothing halfway. She found something fascinating in the tag, in every experience and her enthusiasm was infectious. When she listens, it is with a rapt attention, and an unwavering gaze. It is as if the world is suddenly in sharper focus with brighter colors. Karyn gave me leave to discard my insecurities and buoyed by her wake, every sensation was heightened.

Every minute is right now and every minute lasts forever and ever. There are so many words, but no words for what I am feeling, for what I am seeing. If I was going to allow myself one cliché today, I'd have to say I felt as if the weight of the world had been lifted from my shoulders.

For the first time in a very long time, I relaxed. I could feel the slow breathing of the earth beneath us. I tipped my face upwards towards the sun, feeling I had wings and could fly. Above me pigs are flying and beneath our feet hell is freezing over.

My hand at once clasped hers, almost hungrily. I could feel her joy right away, the hair on my arms went straight out; she was like the electricity that lingers after a thunderstorm. I hugged her body to mine. There should be a bumper sticker, "When was the last time you hugged your lungs?"

Kiss me, I thought, and she did, a kiss, gentle like we had all the time in the world.

I am feasting on life, and thinking of you and your family.

Thank you for the gift of your lungs,

Richard

Friday June 5th – D Day,
The Longest Day, a Day Later
The Other Side

I loaded up the car with all our equipment, Karyn's clothing, and the many photographs that had adorned the walls of her room. Hospital rooms are so sterile-looking with their bare, white-flat-painted walls. Some of us are just like that, dipped in flat, while some of us get dipped in gloss or satin, but every once in a while, you find someone like Karyn who's iridescent and when you do, nothing ever will compare. On the walls, I had placed photos of our granddaughter Avah, our children, our dogs, and Karyn and me. Photos to encourage, to inspire, to move Karyn through the other side.

I drove to Walgreen's to have all the prescriptions filled, a very busy Friday night and a wait of over an hour for Karyn's medicines and drugs. Friday night at Walgreen's was very crowded and all the waiting chairs were taken. Jaws dropped when they saw our load of drugs and paraphernalia, which overflowed the shopping cart.

Then back to the Residence Inn. I unloaded the car, and brought everything in to our home. Karyn sat on the couch resting. I assembled the pieces of the IV tower together, and readied the feed for her nightly dinner. I gathered up the pills and worked to unify the lists from the post-transplant coordinator, the diabetic pharmacist, and the doctors. I was running around chasing my tail, flop sweat on my face. Finally after setting up the GJ tube, I drove to Wendy's down the road for dinner. I ordered and paid for my food and then drove home. My whelm was so over'd, that I forgot my order. Peanut butter and jelly. Just what the doctor ordered. The hours, instead of inching along, seemed almost too short.

We meet tomorrow afternoon with rehab at the Center for Living to set up a program for recovery. The doctors have prescribed all the right medications; it is up to Karyn to do the healing

And for you history buffs, the first insulin shot that I gave Karyn tonight is now the answer to the Shot-Heard Round the World. How many times did I say, I'm sorry?

When I go to sleep, I say one of my special prayers, which I have been saying for years. God bless you Karyn. I love you Karyn. You are my air.

Saturday June 6th

7:00 AM—Karyn's day starts. It should be restful days after a most invasive surgery but for post-lung transplant patients, there is no rest for the airs. Karyn takes her temperature first thing in the morning, and then weighs herself. Blood pressure must be checked thirty minutes later.

8:00 AM—Prednisone, baby aspirin, multi-vitamin, Citracal plus D, Protonix, Septra (with food), Nystatin, Buspar. Before breakfast, blood glucose must be checked (the first of four checks during the day), and then breakfast (which is a thickened fruit drink). Karyn also can take by mouth such foods as applesauce, mashed potatoes, and scrambled eggs.

10:00 AM—Karyn checks her Pulmonary Function Test—the first of two times taking anti-rejection drug, cyclosporine. Before lunch, check blood glucose.

We went for a walk around the complex. Each lap is about a ¼ mile. Karyn did almost a half-mile.

12:00 PM—Rinse mouth with Nystatin, to prevent thrush

2:00 PM—Appointment at DUKE's Center for Living: rehab evaluation, so Karyn can start rehab Monday. She passed all the tests with strength equal on both right and left sides. She also rode the bike for 15 minutes. Rehab on Monday starts at 12:30 and runs to 4:30. Rehab is Monday through Friday

5:00 PM—More pills—Citracal plus D, Valcyte (with food), and Nystatin. Before dinner, check blood pressure, and glucose level.

Karyn's feeding schedule is to take via the GJ tube 960ml of "food" at a rate of 80ml per hour. 12 hours of being hooked up. Yum. No seconds.

10:00 PM—More pills—Protonix, Nystatin, Imuran, Pravachol, and Buspar. Check temperature. Last check of blood glucose.

11:00 PM—Last check of insulin level, 24 hour shot given.

Information on weight, blood pressure, temperature, PFT's, insulin, are all recorded.

It should be that after surgery, your schedule is easy, you sleep a lot, get some strength back, and then add more and more, as you recover. The challenging course for Karyn starts now. Rehab begins Monday. There are also clinic days, where she has to balance everything in her schedule, plus rehab at the Center for Living. First clinic day is Wednesday.

Karyn had her hair washed and blown out at the hair salon this afternoon at 5:15. The birds have left their nest. BTW, this was the first call she had me make when we received the final word that she would be discharged from the hospital on Friday. That's a very good sign.

Richard Schad

Karyn's schedule

Wake-Up
Thermometer—temperature in morning before eating or showering
Scale—weigh first thing in morning after toilet

Thirty Minutes Later (30 minutes after wake-up)
Blood Pressure Cuff

8:00 AM
Prednisone—Take 4 5mg tabs—DO NOT TAKE on clinic days until blood drawn
Baby aspirin—Take 1 81mg tab HOLD FOR 5 days before lung biopsies
Multi-vitamin—Take 1 tablet
Citracal plus D—Take 2 315mg tabs
Protonix—Take 1 40 mg
Septra (with food)—Take one tablet
Nystatin—Take 1 teaspoonful (5 ml) (Wait 15 minutes to eat and brush)
Buspar—Take 1 5mg tab
Before Breakfast
Check blood glucose (insulin checked before each meal and before bedtime)

After Breakfast—check PFT's daily
10:00 AM
Cyclosporine—Take 1 100mg cap and 2 25mg caps

Before Lunch
Check blood glucose

12:00 PM—Noon
Nystatin—swish and swallow

5:00 PM
Citracal plus D—Take 2 315mg tabs
Valcyte—Take 2 450mg tabs(time flexible—take with food)
Nystatin

Before Dinner
Blood Pressure Cuff
Check Glucose Level

10:00 PM
Cyclosporine—Take 1 150mg
Protonix—Take 1 40 mg tab
Nystatin—1 teaspoonful 5 ml
Imuran—Take 2 50mg tabs
Pravachol—Take 1 40 mg tab

Before Bedtime
Check blood glucose level

REHAB – FIRST SESSION
THE OTHER SIDE

Dear Donor,

What will it be like when things get back to their pre-LAM normal? Will there be one day when all of a sudden Karyn is fully healed? Of course not.

But at some point, Karyn should start to feel like her old self, or mostly like her old self before. Before LAM.

Karyn is at her first session of rehab. Her muscles are waking up, especially her back muscles and they are not happy. Her muscles atrophied during her hospital stay. It will take a while for the muscles to wake up. The doctors say recovery takes anywhere from four to eight weeks.

I believe there will come a morning when she will wake up and feel strong. When she feels lousy, with her bloated stomach, feet, and ankles, when the pain electrifies her back, I think about that morning. It can't come soon enough. I put that morning into her hip pocket of her workout clothes to cheer her up. Karyn pretty much cheers herself up, and the moments of sadness are very, very few.

Slowly, Donor, Karyn is becoming Karyn. Simple pleasures like a shower (but she cannot bend down to shave her legs). The steps are tiny, and they pale in comparison to where Karyn saw herself at this point, but she simply modifies her expectations.

Day Won,

Richard

I AM A GLASS HALF-FULL
THIS SIDE

Dear Diary,

People often ask how come I'm always smiling and up. People think that if I might be dying, I would not be positive. Well, I think that's just me. None of us know when the end is coming, but it comes for us all. So making the best of today is important to me.

My son once pointed out to me that when someone would ask how I was, I would respond with a low-key "I'm okay." My son suggested that if I say "I'm great" I would believe it. He was so right. It helped me live each day to my fullest.

Diary, as you know, I have my good days and my bad days. I have cried, been angry, felt alone beyond words. I have my ups and downs. So even though I have those rotten, whiney, I'm feeling sorry for myself days, I know that with or without LAM every day is not a Disney movie with singing birds and frolicking animals.

Anyone, diary, who has a chronic disease and is positive twenty-four hours a day, just does not have both oars in the water. In a perfect world we would all go around thinking only Pollyanna thoughts, but in a perfect world, there would not be LAM or lung disease. Hey, I know I have baggage. We all do. I just have a U-Haul truck.

I remind people that none of us knows what tomorrow holds. Those good people working on 9-11 had no idea that this was their last day. I remind everyone of that, including myself. So just live, live today and then tomorrow, and then there will be, God willing, a yesterday.

I believe that life will really find a way, that I will find a way. I cannot choose what obstacles I will face in life, but I always have the choice in how I deal with them. Sometimes, it is so hard to not let the seemingly endless flow of bad news overwhelm me and make me believe the worst. But even in the darkest of the darkest, when things seem the bleakest, I hold onto my optimism, even if it is a small piece, even if it is just a tiny spark, otherwise I would just give up. I strive, I really do, to be optimistic and uplifted by each day and its possibilities, but I also know there is the very real possibility of some dark days ahead. I do thank God I had a yesterday and hope for another tomorrow. Light, life, love, strength, the will to live, enhanced at each dawn. I feel each day, like when the music is on in the car, on full blast, playing one of my favorite songs, and I push down the accelerator just to do life at full speed. When you feel so hungry for life, you want it all, all at once, now. You want to drink it all up, breathe it all up, every last drop.

I know some things just cannot be changed, some things are inevitable, and then perhaps the only thing that can be changed is me, and my attitude toward such things. There are times when I have no control over what is happening at that moment, but I do have control over how to react to it.

Maybe there was a why and maybe not. It just doesn't matter. Looking for an answer to" why me" is futile, but there are answers to the "what now."

I do recognize the dangers and risks. The beast of LAM is lurking nearby all the time and I prepare as best I can for it. I just do not assume things will turn out well, but I do believe, oh, do I believe, that I can make things turn out well. I do not let the darkness overshadow the light. I like to think that my negative feelings, the whininess, when they come, are merely guests who will visit and leave. Optimism is so dang important—it's too bad doctors cannot give those that do not have it a big booster shot of it.

I am a glass-half-full kind of person, so I can deal with whatever life dishes out, whether it's half full or half empty. Without my bad days, the good ones would not be oh so sweet. I am forever optimistic that tomorrow will contain that moment of joy—that made it all worthwhile getting up. How I love to say tomorrow.

I am a cup half full. I do not think about the what-ifs. I think about the possibilities. I drive a car every day and many more people die from automobile accidents each day than LAM, so would I stop driving? Heck no. Cuz it gets me to the next place. Just like my attitudes do.

But now, Dear Diary, you're thinking I'm not real. In denial. No, you have seen those awful bad days, tears rolling down my face and prayers to God to help me get beyond those moments, and to give me another day. In Judaism, we thank God when we wake, for bringing our soul back to us each morning. I also thank God for allowing me to breathe one more day.

I wonder who first spoke my mantra, yesterday is the past, tomorrow is the future, today is the present, that's why it is called a gift.

I am a glass half full. Top it off with optimism.

Good night diary and thanks for listening,

Karyn

Tuesday, June 9th

Rehab – Center for Living
The Other Side

Dear Donor,

A short distance from the hospital is the DUKE Center for Living, a large workout facility, where Karyn must complete her 23 sessions of rehab.

Each day I drive to rehab, I drop her off in the Center's traffic circle. Cars are backed up, dropping off heart and lung people; all these people getting the most out of their physical conditions. No two alike. To me, it is like an elementary school drop-off zone, a hug and go zone, where I hand Karyn her lunch box (thermos with thickened juice and a soft banana).

Have a good day at school. Play nice with the other kids.

Yesterday was Karyn's first day at rehab. Rehab is Monday through Friday from 12:30 to 3:30, and if transplant classes, to 4:30. Prior to doing the six minute walk (before transplant, it took Karyn ten minutes to do the six minute walk), Karyn had an EKG and when finished with the walk, another EKG. She walked three laps (Thirteen laps or so make a mile), then walked for another 3 minutes. Karyn also did a half hour of floor exercises, weight exercises for the legs (including stair walking) and 20 minutes on the Nu-Step bike. All the time, her vitals are being monitored. Her pulse/ox read 97.

All this on top of getting up at 7:00 AM to start the medical regimen. (Karyn's day does not end until I shovel her into bed at about 10:30, hooked up to her yummy GJ feed bag).

In Ninety-degree Durham weather no one says, "You'll get used to it."

This ain't no dry heat. Instead, the woman cleaning the tables where I set up my lap-top, "I'll tell you what hon, you just sit a spell and wait until it's July, then y'all will taste some holacious hot." I declare.

Where the sun is shining ever-so-bright,

Richard

BAGS. NO BAGGAGE
THE OTHER SIDE

June 9, 2009

Dear Donor,

Over the weekend, I threw out the bags upon bags upon bags of cannulas, tubing, and medicines no longer-to-be-taken. Going through them, I had a big piece of Karyn's LAM treatment.

In those bags, lots of little ways to deal with, and fight against LAM. But what those bags did not hold, could not hold, was her courage. And her strength, and her faith, and her humor, to push back against the LAM. No bag was big enough, strong enough, for those things, it came from her heart.

As I was gathering the bags, Karyn was sitting in a chair, very frustrated, *"I want to feel my new lungs, to share my breath with the person who gave me this gift, this gift of a lifetime."* Sitting there trying with her hands criss-crossed over her lungs, working so hard to feel your lungs. Each precious breath reaching to her new lungs shared with you, her gift-giver.

Karyn is a special soul who shows the rest of us how to embrace life and continue living.

Can I order a bag of Karyn? I betcha there would be a lot of takers.

Karyn shows me time and time again, that a person with LAM, with any disease, is so much more than their physical problems and treatments, so much more than their "Let's stare at the person with the oxygen." So much more than their bags of stuff.

I feel her air and her breath touches my heart.

Donor, thinking of you with each breath,

Richard

WEDNESDAY, JUNE 10ᵀᴴ

UH OH, PFTs DOWN
THE OTHER SIDE

Dear Donor,

After Karyn's early morning regimen, she blows her PFTs around 10:00 AM. The Pulmonary Function Test is done through a spirometer which measures the amount you can blow in one second and the total volume. The FVC volume has been running from 1.36 to 1.55. The FEV1 started out after hospital between 1.25 and 1.34 but in the last few days, dropped to 1.07. A drop of over 10% can be a sign of rejection.

I called the post-transplant coordinator and headed to clinic. Karyn did her PFTs, an ABG, chest x-ray and blood draws. We met with the PA, the doctor, and the dietician. There is not a problem with the PFTs. Thank you Donor. The trach will leak and block the full force of your lungs.

Stitches were removed. About 100 staples! Each staple being taken out feels like a bee sting. Modifications to the protocol were completed, with reductions in the amount of tube feedings and as a result, Karyn's soft foods have now grown immensely, now to include beans, fish, melted cheese, softer fruit, and fully-cooked vegetables. Moosh is the word.

After clinic Karyn and I went to the supermarket. Neither one of us could remember the last time Karyn shopped at a market. We walked around and around the store shopping and then back to the car, parked in a non-handicapped space. Another first in a very long time.

Tonight, I made vegetarian baked beans with melted cheese.

More good news received. The trach will be removed next week at clinic!

Guess who's sleeping now and will have to awakened at 10 for pills, and at 11 for insulin and shot? And when the feed runs out, to be freed of the machine leash around midnight.

I could use a little oomph from your lungs,

Richard

CAREGIVERS, I AM HER LIFELINE AND SHE IS MINE
ON BOTH SIDES

Dear Donor,

It was the best of times. It was the worst of times.

There were so many times that Karyn said, "I just want my life back," but I knew in her wish she also meant, "We just want our lives back." I remember those words said over and over again, "I just want my life back."

Life is the sum total of every moment in whatever those moments unfold for us. The contradiction of LAM is that you perceive the imminent loss of time, but in truth, there is a lifetime to be lived in every minute of every life. Karyn and I chose to live those lifetimes one minute at a time.

Going through the first fifteen years and not knowing what the reason was for Karyn's decline and the ten years of knowing it was LAM, and then the transplant, know this Karyn, "I'd rather be here than anywhere." Also true, "I wish we could be somewhere else."

But, really, what else would I do? Or where else would I be? I am shocked when I hear people say they are surprised and impressed that we are still together. I know that if the tables were turned she would absolutely be there for me. I am her lifeline and she is mine. I guess some just want the wedding and the honeymoon, but not the marriage. Even in this crazy world of ours, I know of no marriage with a pre-nuptial health clause. Marriage and life are not for the wedding vows of "better or worse", but for "better or different." All sales are final. I chose Karyn and Karyn chose me. "Til death do us apart."

When you truly love someone you do not have to think about options, you just do it. Sure LAM and lung disease and the lung transplant were hard on both of us and me as a caregiver, but if you love someone not to give care is unthinkable.

Richard's days are no longer his own—the LAM has stolen those days, changed them from the life he would want to lead to the life he has to lead, a life of caring for me. Karyn, it is not the life I have to lead; rather the life I want to lead.

As a patient Karyn struggled with weakness, fatigue, the loss of who she was—she had to be there, and I get it that we care-givers do not have to be there.

Yes, it was rough on me, but may be rougher on Richard. I pulled my strength from him and he pulled it from me. The family was our strength and I could not have done it without them. Don't send me flowers or get well cards, send them to my husband. He works every day and takes care of me every day too. I truly believe that the caregiver who really loves you has the hardest job in the world. The hardest part of living with LAM was watching my husband watch over me. I am the patient and must deal with the pain and loss, but having to stand by and watch me suffer and knowing there is nothing he could do to stop the loss of my breath, of my pain, of me, is worse. I wish with all my might, that I had not gotten this, not usually for selfish reasons, but because it has changed his life . . . forever. The only people who are as scared as me are my significant others and of course, Richard, my care-giver. Let's face it; LAM is an uncharted road—who knows where it will take me? But the one certainty is, I cannot get through it alone. Cannot. We need others and others need us. I need you Richard.

I sometimes felt that I did not do enough because I wanted to take the LAM away from Karyn and I could not. I wanted to help Karyn through this. But there is no through this.

I remember Karyn taking my hand, and saying. "I know that you are scared and I am sorry." It broke my heart. As caregivers, we have the toughest seat in the house. I may not need to be cured, my body may not be ravaged by disease, but I must find a way to heal.

Each day as a caregiver I live with the same fear. Will Karyn make it through the day? And what about tomorrow?

Sometimes the best thing I can do for my husband, for the others, and for myself, is just to say something very simple. "It's going to be all right." No matter what happens, what is meant to be, I know that is the truth. It is what it is, but that's all it is. Sure LAM was the focus of my life, sure lung transplant was the focus of my life, but it wasn't all there was to life. That there was life before LAM, and there will be life after transplant.

As a caregiver I did what I had to, ignoring my own needs, and in essence giving up my priorities for Karyn. Our study of transplant centers was reduced to a few and UCLA would have been much easier for me, with family and friends in Southern California. I would be able to stay home and work. But DUKE in my opinion was the best choice for Karyn. DUKE favors a double lung transplant, the waiting time was short, the rehab center, the doctors and the surgeons are world class. As a caregiver I must make objective choices, not subjective choices. What is best for Karyn is best for both of us.

Karyn needed me to try to make sense of what is happening. She needed me by her bedside when she could longer tell me I was her husband. She needed me to learn how to give her diabetic shots. To learn how to clean her trach and re-vent her. To feed her through the GJ tube. To push her to walk another lap and then another. To know when it's important to stop talking and just listen. To know when it's important to pull up a chair and sit by the bed and just be there. To know when it's time to hold her hand gently and let her feel the love that flows from my heart to her heart. To laugh with her, and to dry her tears.

Karyn needed me to tell her it will be okay when she knew this may not be true. She needed us to be us. That is the most reassuring thing anyone of us could do. And of course, I need Karyn in all the ways, big and small, that get me through the day. Maybe this is obvious; there are many options when fighting LAM and lung disease, but going it alone is not one of them.

You do need somebody when you are plunked into LAM and Lung world. I had to be strong. I had to make sacrifices for us; willing to move away from home, family, friends and work. I provided care, coordinated our days, drove Karyn to the Center for Living, to doctor appointments, attended lectures, went shopping, carried our heavy loads, did laundry, cleaned up behind us and then sat and waited.

We took it together side by side, down rough roads, and smooth roads, up hills and down hills and even off road. When the mountains looked so high, I wondered how we would ever get over them, and yes, sometimes we did slide off the road into the ditch.

I did what I did to be there, not just for Karyn but for me. I will never be the same person I was before Karyn was diagnosed with LAM and I would not want to be.

I am a napper and look forward to each weekend when I can grab a two-hour sleep in the middle of the day. But I never napped in all the months at Duke. Giving care operates on a 24 hour clock. Sleep when it came, came with one eye open, and both ears trained to hear any sound that was not a sound of the night. How strong I had become; I did not sleep not because of worry but because Karyn needed me to be strong and to help her.

Making a meal, packing lunch for the rehab sessions at the Center for Living, sitting by the bed, just holding a hand. Do anything just to make her day, every day, because you just don't ever know if this will be that fateful last day.

To Pam, To Helene, To Randee, those caregivers who brought me respite and allowed me to return to home and work while taking care of my wife. We start out strong. We figure it's going to be a long haul and we think we can do just about anything to help our loved one through transplant. We're the caregivers. We know our days will change, our routines will be rewritten, but truth be known, we don't have a clue what's ahead of us or for Karyn. We get stronger, because the demands of LAM, of lung disease, of transplant, require us to raise our game. But Pam, Helene, Randee, myself do that because we would do anything, anything at all. We're the caregivers.

Hanging in there as a cheerleader for the most courageous woman that I have ever met was the greatest accomplishment of my life, and I will go to my grave knowing that I will never be a better man than I was during the time I was with my wife, Karyn. I embraced it and performed it to the best of my ability. I will never have any regrets and never have the "I could have done this better" syndrome.

I think it was Hemingway who said that a man is defined not by the way he lived his life, but by the decisions he makes at the apex of stress. We are the sum of our actions in one or two critical testing moments. Some moments were incredibly difficult, but there was also another side to it; it somehow seemed like an amazing privilege to experience the heightened pure love of those days, with everything but love, pain and small comforts stripped away. I would not wish what we went through on another couple, but the intensity of love in those days was a gift we will never ever forget.

While exhaustion and sadness are givens on both sides of the equation, this was also a time of distilled love, and a sparkling clarity of what is most important. The intimacy of caring for my wife brought me to a place of love I could not have imagined and the memories remain most precious.

Hold fast, hold hands, forgive the trespasses.

Blessed be the peacemakers, and even more blessed be the caregivers.

It was the best of times.

It is the best of times.

Thanks for your care,

Richard

Help Wanted: Inquire Within
On Both Sides

Sometimes caring and help from others is hard to take.

We are fed the nonsensical belief in our culture that we all should be independent, all the time. Our culture rewards the doers and the achiever; there are no awards or big salaries for being good at praying or contemplation or meditating. Our culture supports our taking pride in being self-sufficient, so it is very humbling to have that arrogance stripped away when circumstances force us to depend on others for the very basic necessities of life.

I think it comes down to pride. I am not used to asking for help. More times than not, I was the person who others turned to for help; that has changed now with LAM and waiting for transplant. It matters to me that the simplest task can become complicated and difficult. That a trip to the supermarket is daunting. It matters to me that I cannot simply do whatever I want, when I want, and how I want. I have to take big swallows of my pride and realize that my life has changed whether I like it or not. I will be honest with you. I don't like it one little bit. I want to be normal, do normal things, and I hate relying on others. It matters to me I am no longer self-sufficient, and I struggle to sustain my independence, because it acknowledges, at least for me, that LAM and its damage is being kept at bay, at least for the moment.

Karyn, you do not like the way LAM has changed your life, and I, for one, am glad. Not liking it means you have the strength to get a little angry, a little frustrated, and continue the fight and not go gentle into the night. Xanaxers, you hear that?

Staying proud with my bruised pride is yet one more of the challenges. I must accommodate and compromise with my pride. I can no longer take care of my granddaughter. I can only put her on a blanket and place the toys by her. I can no longer pick her up.

I would sing to her even when breathing was so hard—Good night my love, sleep tight my love, may tomorrow be sunny and bright, and may all your dreams come true—it was my gift to her and to me. I can no longer walk my dogs. I can no longer do. It seems all I do is sit in my chair, watch TV and eat.

My loss of control over my life like every loss needs to be mourned. It all comes down to pride and it is tough to give up. Sure part of it is pride, and I just hate to burden others. Everyone tells me what I can do, take it easy, don't overdo it, just relax. But I feel guilty about just lying around and having my husband do everything when he comes home from work. So sometimes I overdo it, but I feel if I can still do the little things, I am going to continue doing them and when I can no longer perform my simple little tasks then I will feel less guilty and let him do things for me.

Karyn had a need to continue her independence as long as possible, and I had to step back and allow her to do those things that she was capable of without hovering, even though it was my absolute joy to be able to help in any way I could. I would try to do things before she asked, and then sometimes she would say that I was hovering, and she would say, "Give me air," and I would laugh.

LAM knocks the stuffing out of you like a scarecrow in a bad windstorm, and as transplant approached, and her strength withered, she was able to accept the situation and accept my help more. My helping did not diminish Karyn in any way. Her gracious acceptance made her appear stronger than ever, a strength that astonished me and her mantle of grace inspired me to be so much more. She had inquired of help within and grace became her.

Which is worse? Having to swallow your pride and ask for help or being the caregiver watching helplessly while seeing the love of your life struggle with the most simple of tasks? I was blessed that Karyn willingly allowed me to help. She gave me a gift by just being with me, and especially by asking me to do things. The opportunity to help allowed me to express my love by doing something. I knew Karyn was fading when she allowed me to wash her red and white underwear, and I was so happy, not coming back with pink panties. I loved preparing her lunch for rehab, picking her up after rehab, taking her to the hairdresser, drawing her bath. Doing. Being. Caring. By receiving, Karyn was letting me feel useful.

Some LAMMIES or LUNGIES cannot overcome the loss of control and the loss of pride. Remember the times when you were there to help others, did you think they were lesser people because they needed help? Did you think they should be embarrassed? I bet not. So do not think of yourself as being lesser because you need help. Accommodate and compromise with being prideful. Being proud is something else—you, like Karyn, have a lot to be proud of.

One of the greatest gifts I can give to others, is to allow them to help me as I need it. Often, if not always, help and assistance is the only thing they have to offer, and they want desperately to help me. I understand completely the pride issue, and I have been found guilty more than once in family court. I have tried to replace the pride with grace, to convey to my family and caregivers, to Helene, to Randee, to Pam, to Susie, to my Richard, and all the others that they are truly making a difference in my life. It helps fill my helpless void.

I draw from your strength Karyn and I am here to help with the heavy lifting. We all need help at one time or another and this was your time.

It took some time to realize I had to learn to receive. I was very comfortable with giving—giving made me feel good—giving led me to a sense of pride. Giving was my legacy and made me happy; taking made me feel bad and it was not me; I somehow felt smaller. But then over time, I realized that I was actually giving while I was receiving—that nice warm feeling I felt when I was the giver was the very thing I was giving to someone else when I was able to graciously receive their help. When I no longer did anything, I extended grace to another person, and we both received a gift.

Sharing is a big part of why we are put on this planet. The ability to accept the caring of others gracefully and gratefully is a mark of personal growth. Humility is the last lesson on the road of life we have to learn, as it leaves us vulnerable. Being able to receive humbly is a greater gift than giving.

We have been told that "It is better to give than receive," but I believe that receiving is a greater gift, to receive is to give.

Allowing others to help you is a way to let people share their gifts with you; holding your hand and helping steady you is a gift. Others want to help you because they care about you. If you are too proud to accept the gift, you are hurting two people. Be ever so patient with yourself, as I know LAM and Lung Disease is not easy.

Being healthy it is sobering to me that one day, if I live long enough, the legs which have been on thousands of hikes and walks will no longer get me out of a chair or across a room without assistance. Hopefully, there will be loving, caring arms to lift me, and hands to hold me, and I will know, like Karyn, that I am receiving the love back I gave to others. Giving is a kind of feedback loop with no beginning and no end.

My wish to all of you caring people in our lives is to help us when we are in need, and the opportunity to help others with a glad heart.

Thursday, June 11th

Cliches
The Other Side

Dear Donor,

As a LAMMIE, you avoid soy. Setting up the feed tube last night, the ISO source is high in soy. Just because you have a transplant, you carry in the back of your mind that LAM is still there, and LAM can migrate from other parts of your body to your lungs. Even when IT'S not there, IT's there.

So today, let's draw a line in the sand. Show those LAM cysts who's in control. Take control of all this. Are there any clichés I've missed?

LAMMIES, let's take the day off! Let's show the LAM cells they don't have power over our lives. Let's not talk about LAM. I'm not going to write about LAM. Let's make those cysts wonder what's going on. Let's show them that they don't have all the power over our lives.

Beware LAM. No L word today.

Sh!

Richard

THE LUNG BADGE OF COURAGE
BOTH SIDES

Dear Donor,

This morning in Durham there was a sunrise made to order, an awakening in a sky that was flecked with pinks and golds and wisps of clouds backlit by the rising sun. Hopeful signs. Did you send them to me, Donor? The fourth day of rehab in the bag. On the way to the magical 23. Who knew 23 was lucky?

There are no rehab sessions on the weekends. I wish there were, as does Karyn, but I know she does need a break, and healing also takes time, not just the 23 days at rehab.

I so hope your family is healing.

I asked Karyn if facing a lung transplant and the recovery and always knowing that she must protect your lungs, made her courageous. Lung transplant surgery is like being run over by a Mack truck, and like no other transplant, is always exposed. Every time you take a breath, Karyn exposes your lungs. Karyn, of course, said off-handedly, "*No.*"

I found Karyn a year or so before her transplant on the floor of our upstairs bedroom closet, unable to catch her breath after simply trying to dress herself. How do you manage a simple smile when you cannot get enough breath to dress yourself and all you want to do is curl up in a corner and cry? *Sobs came, heavier now, racking my body, slicing through me like hot blades. To breathe or not to breathe, that is the question. Such an easy thing to do, but for me it was almost impossible. I never imagined the big achievement of my day would be getting off the floor.*

Life had become a mortal struggle, the tank by her side and the cannula in her nose; they were both her friends and her enemies.

Courage, I have learned, comes in many forms. There is courage on the battlefields of Afghanistan and Iraq, courage to speak out, courage to stand up for what you believe. All of those are very real. But I am talking about a very different kind of courage I think Karyn and the LAMMIES and the Lungies have and show each and every single day. Sometimes just getting off a closet floor, just taking the next step on a long journey, putting one foot in front of the other is an act of true courage. Sometimes it takes courage just to get through the moment and face another test in the next moment.

Karyn stared down LAM, the schoolyard bully. *Lung disease is a bully with such a bad reputation that they no longer have to fight. Just the mere thought of it can send people running away.* But all it takes are the Karyns to stand up to the bully, to diminish their reputation. That's what Karyn did; she stared down the bully. Anyone can give up—it's the easiest thing in the world to do. But to hold it together when everyone else would understand if you fell apart, that's true courage.

To me, a coward is someone who runs away, who fails to act out of fear. For many lungies, fear takes up residence in their brains; a most unwelcome guest. No LAMMIE patient is a coward, no lung patient is a coward for one very simple reason. They are not allowed to be. How many LAMMIES or Lungies would love to run away from their disease? From the treatments, the pokings in every orifice, the ABG's, the medications, the side effects, the discomfort, the pain? I believe at some point, all have felt that. Agreed? But it's just not an option. They cannot run away. You cannot run away. So they are left with one and only one choice. Stand and face it.

Most people are never tested, never ever having to reach down inside themselves to find courage to do the simplest things. Those who are tested in ways they never expected, find something within themselves that they did not know was there. Their bravery takes my breath away.

The courage of Karyn and others faced with LAM and the untold myriad of lung disease; is not the kind of courage that is ever recognized. There are no medals, no parades, no invites to the White House, and rarely does anyone around them, stop to think about it.

Guess I have gotten used to feeling bad. I am not feeling sorry for myself, but you just get used to your new realities, good or bad—and it is always amazing what you can get used to—that's when you find out how strong you are, not when you are going through a crisis, but when you have to keep going through it, day after day after day. When no matter how tough the previous day was, you have to get up and do it all over again—that's when courage comes in—so maybe one day I will wake up and feel better. I do not count on it; I just hope each day that things will not get worse and I tell myself that no matter how hard, I can do it. This does mean it will be easy, but I hope there won't be any surprises. I could use a no surprise day.

Every step I take is a mountain I conquer. I can do this, one step at a time, one breath at a time. Just give me a minute to catch my breath.

Courage of the donor's family. Courage, when confronted with challenge, courage in the face of fear; to live the day, not the LAM. Inner courage is a powerful thing to witness. All I can say is Phew. Double Phew.

You can be brave, but that does not mean you do not get scared. Sure LAM scared Karyn. Sure the lung transplant scared Karyn. LAM scared her pretty much on a daily basis. But made Karyn a coward? Never.

Karyn and I do not know what the next moment will bring. It could bring defeat. LAM and the multiplicities of lung diseases, make us more aware of how fragile our lives truly are, and why we need to use our time ever so wisely; nothing cowardly about facing that.

Though we may feel like cowards, we are strong, but LAM and lung diseases, if anything make us stronger. We are all like the cowardly lion in the Wizard of Oz—all we want is courage and then we find we had it.

The sheer act of being here today, Karyn's grace in how she accepts this reality, that truly defines her character. Karyn and your lungs had already won so much more than a medal.

When I help Karyn in the shower this morning, I see her main incision line, which swings horizontally across her chest, under her breasts, a clam-shell opening. The cut is fairly discrete preserving her bikini line (like she is ever going to wear a bikini again), and designed so the surgeon could lift her rib cage up, to access the lungs. There are slashes where the chest tubes were inserted to support your lungs, while they expanded to occupy the new space. Small nicks from venous lines inserted at various points, bruises from needle encounters, Karyn does look battered as if she survived a shark attack. I will always see these scars as badges of her courage, of your courage.

Maybe her scars are like a tattoo Karyn can look at and say there is a history there, a story to be told. Maybe her scars are tattoos with better stories to tell.

All our scars are earned and paid for, I suppose.

May I be as brave as you and your family,

Richard

IT TAKES A LOT OF PATIENCE TO LEARN PATIENCE
THE OTHER SIDE

Dear Donor,

We walked ½ mile early on Sunday morning and were planning on a much longer walk in the evening, but we had received a call from the post-transplant coordinator regarding a bronch scheduled for tomorrow afternoon, so the feeding start had to be moved up, eliminating our nighttime stroll. Flexiblity is the watchword in the post-transplant world. Patience for all the changes.

Karyn is still stuck at four days of rehab. This Monday morning back at the hospital for a bronch, she was put under into dreamland. She also had her lungs tapped, with some fluids removed. The doctor proclaimed, "The lungs look good." Thank you, thank you, thank you. "You should not operate heavy machinery, drink alcohol, swim, skateboard, or use roller blades." Karyn giggled to me, *"That just means I will have to return the front loader to John Deere."*

Karyn's silver choker trach was removed and covered with a gauze bandage. The hole in her neck will take two to three weeks to heal over.

Tomorrow morning we meet with the speech therapist and more swallowing tests. Hopefully, Karyn will do well and get an up-grade in her diet. Last night, due to the scheduled bronch and no "food" after midnight, we started the GJ feed tube earlier, so Karyn could sleep without being umbiloco'd to the IV tower. Another giggle from Karyn, *"Yippee, what a treat, I can actually turn over in my sleep."*

Patience is so very hard when you can see the light at the end of the tunnel, and being able to go home. But we do know if we are always taking our temperature to see if we are happy, we won't be happy. I guess it's like watching the clock; nothing can happen if all I am doing is watching the seconds tick off.

I remember on weekends, when I was young, I would walk with my cousin, Ron, to the local corner store, Akins Grocery, and spend pennies on an all-day sucker. It would not have lasted all day, but it could last a long while. The trick was to resist the temptation to bite into it, learn to savor rather than to crunch and chew. Stretch out the sweetness. I am a biter, and sometimes I just wanted to bite.

Without patience, we learn less in life, we feel less. Ironically wanting to rush and bite usually means less. Patience is bitter, but its cherry fruit is oh so sweet.

The problem with becoming patient is that you cannot practice it without being put in a situation that requires it. I am not a patient patient. We in Lung Land face the unexpected delay, the wait for lungs, the time in the hospital, the days of rehab. But then we fall totally under the domination of time, allowing the calendar to drive us, rather than calmly living in the richness of the moment.

To those waiting at rehab, you will have new lungs from someone as kind as our donor: and to those who have been transplanted, you have new lungs, and you can breathe. (Insert deep breaths here).

Karyn and I look to Patience as a guide, a time to heal, a time to form strong bonds, moments that take our breath away, Breaths of life.

Listening yesterday to my car radio and Symphony Pops and John Williams, and Star Wars, life cannot all be kettle drums and crashing cymbals. Living cannot all be crescendo. If only it could, but there must be violins, and flutes, a balancing counter-point.

There is a message in the lollypop for me to grow and to perfect myself. Thanks to you, Donor, Karyn and I can lick all things together.

I hear my grandmother's words that patience is to be treasured, that patience carries a lot of wait. We feel the wait. I need to be patient and that may be one of the biggest challenges yet.

We are trying to be patient. Lord, please give me patience, but can you hurry it up? Both of us want to bite into the lollypop.

With ever-growing love and deep admiration,

Richard

Tuesday, June 16th

So What's Chew
The Other Side

Dear Donor,

Karyn and I drove in early this morning to the DUKE South Clinic for her up-dated swallow tests. This time we were prepared for the green yuck and brought toothpaste and a toothbrush. You know what Kermit said, "It's not easy being green." A camera is inserted down Karyn's nose to the vocal cords, and she is given different items to swallow in different ways other than a brief pause on the tip of the tongue, probably caused by the brain telling Karyn how to swallow correctly. Karyn passed with flying green colors. I am sure Kermit is very proud.

The clinician will up-date Karyn's records and recommend full diet other than hard breads, and crackers. We see the doctor late tomorrow at clinic, and I presume Karyn will be on a full-food diet at that time. I am not sure how this works with the feedings at night. Karyn just loves her feedings at night. (Yeah, right). The GJ is very uncomfortable, knotting in her stomach and forcing her to eat even smaller portions of currently-allowed foods.

We will also be at clinic early tomorrow morning so she can do the litany of tests, including the ABG, blood draws, chest x-ray, and PFTs. Tomorrow, we will get the results of the biopsy of her lungs taken yesterday during the bronch. The test determines what, if any, rejection is occurring.

Last night, we walked ¾ of a mile, the greatest distance Karyn has walked. I am a harsh taskmaster and this is not hard to swallow.

Clouds have gathered beneath a bruised and purpled sky, much like Karyn after the surgery. In the growing darkness now, the sky is the color of charcoal and the air thick with the possibility of summer rain. A fine silver rain, like cobwebs falling. Thousands of hands began tapping on the roofs. Large droplets spattered the window, hung for a bit, and then joined by others, slid down the window pane. The rain and sky rumble away, like the growls of a predator stalking its prey. The rain has subsided to a soft mist that seems to dance in the early summer twilight. A light mist broke through the gray sky, unleashing streams of pure sunshine, like our own personal sunbeam. The rhythm of the wind blends with the rain. We take a deep breath and the cool dampness of the nearby trees fills our lungs.

Every breath we take,

Love, Richard

THE OTHER SIDE

Dear Donor,

Wednesday June 17th

Karyn walked one mile in 20 minutes at rehab. Her PFTs were significantly up. The bronch did not show any signs of rejection. No bronch needed until two months from now. A great early father's day present!. Thank you Donor.

Karyn is off the feed tube and has an open diet. Off for a burger and fries for the young lady.

Thursday Karyn walked one and one/third mile in 30 minutes and without realizing or exerting herself, walked a mile Friday. At rehab, she also worked the weights, the Nu-bike stair-stepper and floor exercises.

Two weeks out from the hospital and the Karyn of new is becoming more and more the Karyn of old.

Parking in regular spaces at the mall. Walking throughout the mall. No more handicap parking. The malls are alive celebrating your lungs in Karyn.

Tell God I love you,

Richard

"Take Your Best Shot"
On Both Sides

Friday June 19, 2009

When I was home for a week in May, I ended up downstairs in storage looking for a book, and instead came across an old box of even older photographs of Karyn when she was a child. One faded shot popped back into my mind yesterday: It was one of Karyn, age 6 or 7, cradling under her arm one of those inflatable punching bags. Remember those inflatable punching bags we had as kids? You'd hit one as hard as you could, it would fall back, and then pop right up to take another shot. I had a bag like that also; most of those bags had clown images on them, although I don't know why someone thought it was a good idea to teach us kids to beat up clowns.

But that's sort of what it's like to be a LAM, or lung patient. You get kicked in the gut, fall down, and then pop up again, ready for the next shot. At least you try to be ready. You take your bronch and hopefully in the next few days, the findings show there are no signs of rejection. You go active on the list and wait and wait and wait like our good friend, Gene, has done for over 50 days. You fight through three weeks of ICU like John is doing. You battle through "stroke like symptoms" as Karyn did. You go back on oxygen after your transplant like Robert is doing—fall back like the clown to bounce back to go forward.

You're out of breath. You're on the vent. You're put on the trach. You have to take your medications and nutrition through the GJ tube. You're back on the vent. You go to clinic and then go home to take your meds and shots, and then you come back for rehab, and then you drive to clinic to meet the doctor. You go for more shots and meds and the feed bag.

You're like Barbara who spent a month in the hospital, out for two weeks, and then back to the hospital with an infection. No matter how you are feeling, you just learn to take the next punch.

I sit watching from my perch nearby the Duke Center For Living, the home of good 'ol fashioned barbecued rehab, those men and women, who struggle up the walks to the entrance, many of their frames bent and battered. There should be a statue out front of the CFL proclaiming, "Give me your poor of oxygen, your huddled masses with walkers, yearning to breathe free."

I am the boxing trainer, standing off to the corner of the Living Center ring, watching, cringing, imagining that I can feel the pain of the huddled masses fighting the good fight. In a weak moment today, I look away as one gentleman takes 10 minutes to walk 10 feet; it looks so brutally hard. Even Bill Clinton drawls, "I feel your pain". But then I realize what that means—that I do not believe in my fighter; that I may not be sure that this fighter in my string can take so many hits. It means I might have doubt. It means admitting just how hard it is for me to helplessly watch. So I regain my composure and once again begin to root my fighters on. You can do it, take that rehab, give them the 'ol one-two. Take that LAM. Take that Pulmonary Fibrosis; an uppercut to CF. Hit them in the 'ol COPD.

Then comes those quick, highly stressful moments in between rounds when I have the privilege, the responsibility, to look into the eyes of my fighters. To wipe their sweat, blood and tears. To be in their corner when their temperature goes up, when their PFTs go down, when infection or rejection may be appearing, when the GJ tube contorts their stomach, when the lightning jabs of pain strike. I tell my boxer how strong she looks, how she is bigger and better than the opponent, and will without a doubt emerge victorious. And then, when my fighter and the other fighters in my string go back in for yet another round, and the noise of the crowd in my head is so freaking loud, I hope that no one can see my agony, my tears, but it is seen.

I so want to walk with them, but it is their journey, their fight. Actually, I think I want to carry them all. The worst part for me, is the person I want to support; she is the person who has a much bigger fight to fight.

I am exhausted watching each one of them stride up to the Living Center, each step of the struggle, but they do, step after step, step after step, and all with an easy and amiable smile. Each one of them, like the punching bag, keeps popping back up punch after punch. Each one with the smile of that clown.

Whatever issues they have, they sure as hell aren't going to make it easy for the diseases or the post-transplant regimen to get them down. I remember that after enough punches and kicks, those inflatable clowns usually sprung a leak, and deflated for good. Down for the count. It ain't how many times you're knocked down, it's how many times you get up. Clown, stay down. Fighters, get up.

As Karyn fights through the knock-downs, and gets up each morning, it is indeed an honor, a privilege to work her corner through each round. To give her water, a pep talk between rounds, to soothe her wounds.

Dear Donor,

Rehab three hours. 6th day of rehab (But who's counting?). Karyn came out of the PFT lab this morning with a smile shinier than Ali, a smile as wide as the Grand Canyon. PFTs were the best yet, FVC was 1.92, .61 per cent of predicted, a big jump over .50 last week. FEV1 was at 1.51, her best score yet. This means as your lungs expand, that Karyn's oxygen capacity will grow and grow (this process can take up to a year). All three judges ringside on their cards declare her the undisputed champion. Her arms go straight up in the air she is breathing, declaring a unanimous victory today. Take that clown.

Love,

Richard

A SURVIVOR BY ANY OTHER NAME, SO FAR

BOTH SIDES

Dear Donor,

Is survivor the right word? The right name? I have "survived" and lived life so far, but when I think of survivor, I think of someone who has been through it, and has gotten past it, once and for all. It seems the words, "so far" should always be tacked onto the word Survivor. I have LAM still, and I take serious anti-rejection drugs, so am I a survivor? I take tons of pills and medications and shots for diabetes. None of us can ever really know what the cells of our body may be doing.

LAMMIES, and all those with a chronic disease, every day after your diagnosis that you continue to live and breathe and love, you are survivors. Today you got up, you are a survivor. If you are reading this in bed, then today you woke up and that makes you a survivor. Sometimes, not too long ago, staying in bed is all that I could do—sometimes I couldn't do more than just sit in a chair and read a book, watch TV, or just sit. Those are tough days.

When I talk about living life, it does not mean that you always have to be at your best, that you're the life of the party. It does not mean you're out climbing Mt. Everest or learning to play Mozart concertos on the piano or biking the Appalachians—that's not it at all. I think that the best that any of us can do is appreciate each day that we have, even the bad ones. You may be overwhelmed by the pain or the hurt, or the taking away of what you once could do, but do the best you can and get through the day in the hopes that tomorrow may be better.

LAM and lung disease are relentless. LAM and lung disease do not lose a battle here and there and then give up though I wish they did. I wish all you had to do was kill a LAM cell or two, and then the LAM would throw up its hands and say okay, you win, but we all know better. LAM never gives up. Now that does not mean we give up either. I think it means at some point the LAM may win or the rejection of the transplant may win. Until a Cure is found.

LAM and lung disease do not have a brain or a heart or a spirit. LAM cannot plan or be cunning. LAM does not have a heart that causes it to fight or a spirit that gives it the heart to fight. We who have the brain, the ability to strategize; we have the soul and the heart to fight.

I wear my survivorship as a badge of honor for all to see, so others will not be afraid to fight the bully of LAM or lung disease.

If survivor is not the best word, what about victim? That's probably closer to the mark. I did not do anything to get this disease: Just happened to my body, besieged by LAM or a lung disease. LAM took from me like a thief, robbing me of so many things—running, dancing, stealing my breath away. But when I say victim, that does not mean LAMMIES are weak or passive, that LAMMIES just sit by and let this happen. Everyone I know who has LAM does not go quietly into the night; they are not weak or passive. They are not giving into the disease and victim does not mean helpless.

I think victim is old terminology. I don't care much for the word, because it makes one sound passive and well, like a victim. Victims do not have a say in their fates and are doomed in stories. I know victim is a loaded word. I am not a victim; I am one of a number of strong women who have LAM.

Is "LAM patient" a better choice? It is accurate in a bland sort of way. It really does not get across what's it's like to have LAM, what we all go through. It makes it sound too easy, too clean. Patient is an apt description as we have to be very patient. Wait for the results of tests. Wait to catch our breath. Wait to see how the disease progresses. Wait.

Maybe seizer is a better word. A seizer is pretty busy, yet anyone at any stage of LAM or lung disease can seize. I seize moments in the day, along with new and old relationships. I seize new treatments, new clinical trials, new protocols. I seize all hopes and dreams. I have seized on nature on walks. I have seized on my family and friendships. I have seized on the moment.

I know the truth is I am not surviving a darn thing, because I along with you will one day, die. But, today, I seize, therefore I am.

I am a person who has LAM, ready to seize everything. I can seize before LAM, or whatever else seizes life from me. Hail Seizer.

Then again, maybe coper is a better term. I'm not sure that's a real word. I cope with stuff. I cope with things that I never thought I'd be able to. I cope with things that I wouldn't wish on my worst enemy. I get through it. I am a coper.

I wish for a survivor's miracle, but in lieu of that, may you cope well with your LAM, or your lung disease, and that which you seize can be miraculous.

I think that's what our future is, and the future for all of us. We're going to cope with whatever hurdles the lungs put in front of us. We'll get through it. And if the future isn't exactly what we had planned, if it's not what we daydreamed about, well, we can cope with that also. Copers, we are. As Richard's Grandma Sarah use to tell me, it isn't the load that breaks us down, it's the way we carry it.

Does it really matter what term we use? I guess how we define ourselves says a lot about how we face this disease, but in the end, I think we are all just people who happen to have gotten a disease. What more do I need to say?

LAM shows us that living is a verb. LAM is an action word. Surviving, seizing. coping, seeing, doing, feeling, saying, touching, smelling, tasting. It is climbing and occasionally falling. LAM and lung disease is not a waiting word. Do not wait to live. Starting right now, seize every minute out of each and every day. Copers, we are.

If you do, you'll realize the way I live; that each and every day well-seized is a miniature lifetime.

I know that there's no such thing as a bad survivor or coper or seizer or patient. All of us—that's all of us—are just muddling through this, so even on bad days, when you can't catch your breath, doing the best you can, and saying that you're going to try again tomorrow, that's a triumph. Savor it.

Ultimately, the perfect survivor is you, simply, because you have survived. So far.

To tomorrow,

Karyn

August 28, 2009

Survivor's Guilt
The Other Side

When two transplanted lung patients or two LAMMIES meet, a momentary flicker passes between their eyes as if to say, "I know, I've been there, and I have come out The Other Side."

It is like watching my father who was a hero in World War II at Normandy and the Bulge, greeting another Purple Heart or Silver Star. It is said that old soldiers never die nor ever tire of reliving the glories of their battles or of the loyalties of their comrades, both the fallen and the survivors.

As the women against the battle of LAM and those transplanted, and those with a lung disease, this is a battle that you will always be proud to have fought. To have shared with those who fought with you, those both living and fallen, for you have learned as every soldier does, that it is not necessarily the outcome that matters, it is having risen to the fight that counts.

On The battlefield of DUKE, the rush after the shots and the episode stopped, and the guns silent, and I felt more alive than I have ever been before. It's the sheer joy of seeing my wife survive. My sensations are sharper, and the air is crystalline clear. It's only afterwards that it sinks in that not everyone makes it, not everyone survives. That's where survivor's guilt comes in.

When someone is diagnosed with LAM or another lung disease, one of the first questions wrestled with is "Why me?" "Why was I singled out?" "Why am I sick when others are not?" But it's not very long before we realize that this is the wrong question. Why not me is just as fair. There really are no answers to either question. Why is not the question. We have LAM. We have lung disease. We have to deal with it. We have to look ahead.

Why was Karyn so lucky? Why has Karyn gotten a break when so many others have not? Why can't we all survive?

I guess I have some guilt, though it's not really guilt, it's more a feeling of profound deep sadness, not for myself but for all of you who have not gotten good news, who are not going to beat this, even for a little while. There was not an answer to why me in the beginning and there is no answer now.

Don't get me wrong. I am thrilled that I am here today and Karyn is alive. I do not know what is in the future. None of us does. But through this ordeal we have all been walking the same road, shoulder to shoulder. We all faced the same fears, the same challenges, the same heartbreak and we all learned lessons we could not have learned any other way.

This is probably going to sound a little silly, but I feel guilty about being here. I know how truly lucky I am, not just to be here with my wife, but to be here at all. But as I sit here writing, it's hard for me to stop thinking about all of you who are having a tough day, sitting in the waiting room, or at home, which in spite of the familiar comforts, can seem so darn lonely sometimes. I know what you are going through and yet I'm not going through it, and that feels strange to me.

I feel like I have stepped at least partway out of the LAM and lung world. My guilt is like a virus and it's always on my mind. Friends bump into Karyn, "It's great to see you here." Of course, that sentence can be read in a couple of different ways and they mean them all.

So what am I feeling? Survivors guilt? That's part of it certainly.

Why me? I am no more worthy. I wish I could bring you all to where I am today.

Survivor's guilt. There should be no such thing. Instead there should be survivor's anger.

We're mad as hell we have not all made it. Yet.

Miracle of Miracles – 2 Lungs, 1der of Wonders

On Both Sides

Tuesday June 23, 2009

Dear Donor,

Albert Einstein, who knew everything was relative, believed that there were two ways to live—nothing is a miracle and everything is a miracle.

Thank you donor, for the gift of breath, for the gift of life, for the gift of every moment. To be able to breathe again, to taste the air throughout my body after so many years is a miracle. I devour life, savoring every bite. I know that every miracle you get to keep becomes normal, but I still feel a magnificent sense of wonder that I can breathe.

The feeling I get when I go to sleep, and when I wake up in the morning that everything is all right in the world, that amazing feeling that I am whole, that I have got everything I want, and that I am not missing anything. I know tomorrow will be an unforgettable day.

I believe in a lot of unbelievable stuff. How can I pick and choose which miracles make sense and which do not? Miracles may not make sense and sometimes miracles do not look like you'd think they would. Sometimes we might not even recognize them.

Sitting in my wheelchair with my trusty IV tower by my side, in the DUKE Alcove garden, the first time "outside" after my transplant I hear the song of the Cardinal. The song of the birds, the smell of the flowers, the outside, has not made the discomfort and pain go away, (that would be a miracle), but it's a reminder that no matter what's going on with me, life goes on. I hear the chirping of the birds and for a couple of minutes it made me smile, and on a day like this that's invaluable.

Miracles come in all shapes and sizes. When I hear the birds sing, it always makes me smile. These birds have been singing since the beginning of time, for centuries and centuries, through war and peace and everything in between. They are a blessed constant and I am reminded that someone is watching over them and me, through all times.

Words move through me, but they do not come from me. Not a voice, not a burning bush, just a sense, a hint of presence, that all will be okay and that I am not alone. Faith in miracles. Faith just isn't faith until it's all you are holding onto.

I am outside, breathing without supplemental oxygen, and have just received the miracle of life, the miracle of your double lung transplant. Many people still are astounded, "They can do that?" "They can give you new lungs?" The way I see it the impossible happens all the time, but we are so good at taking it for granted, we forget it was once impossible.

I do believe miracles happen every day. I think people often forget the miracle of life and for me, the second chance of life. I work hard not to be overwhelmed with every mundane task, and responsibilities, and just remember the true blessing of the Life that you gave to me.

Life is about living, gratitude, joy, passion, happiness, excitement, joyful expectations, hope, and satisfactions. Sure there are ups and downs in life, but this is my life and my second chance at a healthy, happy, and loving life.

You know what's best of all? Your lungs.

A miracle says I am worth a miracle.

In between breaths,

Karyn

When something is taken from you, you realize what a gift of giving it was, and so sometimes, many times, I just watch Karyn breathing. One breath at a time, and another, and another, until she catches me staring. Oops, caught again.

Thank God for A Coincidence
Both Sides

Dear Donor,

Do you believe in destiny, or fate or divine providence? Being at the right place at the right time, something random, or God's plan?

Everything happens for a reason they say, and I am not sure who they are, but that's what they say. I hear people say that nothing is coincidence or everything happens for a reason. Everything does happen for a reason, doesn't it? Life is made up of so many coincidences that sometimes we simply take them for granted.

My goal was to stay alive long enough to go and enjoy my son's wedding in August of 2008. I think that goal is pretty common. We set goals for ourselves, a wedding, a birthday, a graduation, a holiday, a family get-together—some event we are going to live long enough to enjoy. What keeps us going?

It's not like we're all given the choice of what we want to live to see, but I do think willpower plays a huge part. I do not think it's a coincidence that like me, so many people live long enough to see that wedding or graduation. I also do not think it's a coincidence that once those deadlines have been reached, people often pass away or their disease gets worse. My oxygen levels decreased dramatically after the wedding.

Even at the wedding my dance with my husband was him standing in front of me, while I slightly swayed to the music and then had to immediately sit down, exhausted, short of breath. Merely standing up had become an aerobic exercise.

I agree that the will to live, the will to believe, to enjoy, to see or reach milestones is powerful but it could be easy to slide down the slippery slope of "If she just had more willpower, she could have lived longer." This is just as absurd as believing that if you fight hard enough you can beat the LAM down, or not have it show up for dinner in the first place.

I guess what keeps us alive is different for everyone. How about my new lungs letting me live long enough to see the cure for LAM? It reminds me of the old joke about the dying woman who made a deal with God, that she will live to see her daughter married. She does, and then God comes for her, and she tells God, "But God, I have four more daughters."

I remember you, Karyn, from the teenage youth camp in March 1965, when you were with my friend, Eric. I love that I can bring up that picture in my head anytime I want. I remember you at that dance in December of 1965. Your every movement flirted with me, or did it? You spoke to my friends and me after the dance at the top of the stairs as you were leaving. How is it that my friends and I were just standing outside after the dance? After a dance, we just left. You asked us if we knew Eric, and when we said yes, we asked you how you knew Eric, and you smiled, "Come to my dance next week and I will tell you." Her words were like a joy-filled helium balloon, lifting me up. God, I was captivated. Was there a magnet inside her drawing me into her orbit? The butterflies, the heart flutters. I knew I had seen forever in a second, in a split second, in the split of a split. The spell has never been broken.

It's no coincidence. I remember leaving the dance and looking out the backseat passenger window up to the sky, counting and pointing, 1, 2, 3, 4, 5, not realizing I was speaking out loud. My buddy sitting next to me, asked me what I was mumbling. I was too shy to reply. I was counting my lucky stars

The idea that our paths might just as easily not have crossed leaves me breathless, like a near-miss accident on the highway and I can't help marveling at the sheer randomness of it all. I feel a quick rush of thankfulness, part adrenaline, part hope, and all God.

Through the years, I was deathly afraid of doctors and hospitals. One of my friends was in the hospital; as I visited him, I hyperventilated and my blood pressure skyrocketed into the 200's. White coat fever would cause my thermometer to boil over. Karyn would travel every six months to the National Institutes of Health as part of their LAM protocol. I would ask on her return, "What did the doctors say? She would say, "Look at this picture of a dog who came to visit me." "What did the doctors say?" "Look at this picture of another dog, who came to visit me." "Isn't she cute?" Somewhere in the recesses of my brain, the talk of dogs providing pet therapy stuck. Then, due to her LAM and avoiding getting her sick, and catching a cold, she had me attend the local senior fair to get a flu shot. On the way out past the exhibits, there was a woman at the end of the table with her dog. I stopped and chatted and asked her what they did. She and her dog visited patients at Exempla Good Samaritan Hospital. She told me about pet therapy and I started on the journey that led my two dogs and me into many hundreds of hours visiting patients at the hospital, and my white coat fever disappeared, the thermometer sang 98.6, and I could be at my wife's side for her double lung transplant. Coincidence?

As my wife was awaiting transplant, I signed up for the orientation class at our local transplant agency, The Donor Alliance. I wanted very much to speak out and spread the gospel of donating one's organs. Karyn was not coming to the class, as the walk from the car was a marathon distance for her, and she was fighting still another cold. On the morning of the class, Karyn let me know that she thought she should come to the class, as the reason I was going was for her.

After the moderator spoke for a while, we went around the class introducing ourselves and why we were here. The third member of the class introduced himself as Gavin, who had had a double lung transplant at DUKE. Karyn had been told by one of the nurses at University Hospital to talk to Gavin, as he had been rejected by University Hospital and chose to go to Duke. Karyn had been active on the University list for 30 months and there was not one call. Months and months and months had passed and Karyn had not spoken to Gavin. When it was Karyn's turn to talk, she ended her talk with, "Gavin, I need to talk to you afterwards about Duke." I discovered after this class that as I did not donate or received organs, I could not be a speaker, but rather someone who would set up booths or hand out brochures—not my cup of tea. Had I known, I would not have attended, and Karyn would not have met Gavin and set the final journey of transplant to Duke. Coincidence?

I believe there are no coincidences, only the illusion of coincidences. Sometimes, we are like race horses, fitted with our own blinders. Our blinders are invisible and most of the time we do not even know they are there. We forget to see outside the blinders, outside the lines. We simply do not notice. Sometimes we even do not see what is right in front of our face. I think there are signs of God's hand all around if we just know where to look.

If you see these items as more than random luck or quinky dinks or just plain luck, as I do, then open the door a crack to new possibilities. It makes you more humble, less discontented and so very full of gratitude. The random is so random, it cannot be mere randomness. You know, sometimes God opens his palm and hands us a gift, a Godly green light.

I wonder, was it purely coincidence I was given the lungs I received or did God lay out his plan between you, my donor and me even before my lifetime?

It could be said that all of life is random or just plain luck, and everything somehow does connect, but this does not explain these and other stories, which seem so artfully scripted as if one can imagine a master story teller. Who else but God?

After all, I know nothing is coincidental

It is no coincidence that I am writing my story, our story, donor. Coincidences are merely God's way of remaining anonymous.

Coincidentally, one thing does not lead to another, it leads to everything.

I was right where I was supposed to be at just the right time. I was right where I was supposed to be at just the right time.

WEDNESDAY JUNE 24, 2009

THE OTHER SIDE

10 days of rehab completed. Clinic today, so no rehab. The clock stays at 10 days. All clinic tests went well.

The PFT's were somewhat lower, but this is normal. The watchword we hear all the time, "It's not unusual."

Karyn is doing so well, that the pulmonologist suggested no clinic next week, but Karyn requested labs next week, but no doctor consult, so there will be no down time from rehab (other than one day stomach acid reflux test).

Thursday June 25, 2009
The Other Side

The oxygen tanks were picked up; the umbilical cord has been cut. The trach supplies, the ventilator, the tubing, the concentrator. The oxygen was a blessing in Karyn's past, and that is what it is now, her past.

THE FIRE WITHIN KARYN
BOTH SIDES

Dear Donor,

I am sitting in the front room of our Residence Inn home, which serves as family room, den and eating area, staring at the fireplace, wishing it was cold enough for a fire, just daydreaming.

When logs are first set ablaze, a small gradual fire ensues; Karyn and I freshly dating in 1965, a fire moving like an infant crawling, both of us learning to walk on our own. The flame grows ever-larger, and burns more briskly. Karyn growing past her teenage years, experiencing life, gaining knowledge, and growing into womanhood. We are oh-so-young and pulse to pulse. You can feel the heat like two boy-scout sticks rubbed together. There's a reason kissing in my parent's day was called sparking.

The fire peaks, and the logs emerge into roaring flames. The fieriness of romance and early marriage, raising our children, starting a career, the pace of life ever-so-fast. Keeping life on track consumes all of our time. There never seemed enough hours in the day. Always another bill to pay, another appointment, another schlepping of kids to a school or sports event. Like the fire roaring, life is warm and it is satisfying. But somehow I got bogged down in the details and I forgot we are living it.

And then, before I realize it, the logs begin a slower, more gradual burn, our children grown and out on their own, and life slows to a gradual, more peaceful pace. We are older and I wonder how we have walked this enormous distance in so short a period of time. Somehow I got bogged down in the details, and I forgot we are living it.

Then 10 years ago, Karyn's fire was engulfed by LAM, she burning out and turning cold, her face like dying embers, turning ashen gray. Somehow, I got bogged down in the details, and forgot we were living it.

God, in his tender mercy, miracle of miracles, placed another log on the fire. The fireplace simmers the red-hot coals awake, and we only need to stir the coals for that extra flame, and another cord of happiness, excitement and life. I spread my hands over the rekindled fire to warm my hands, my heart and my soul, from the fire that stirs anew within Karyn. Your lungs, Donor, are the bellows and oxygen, and air once again fan, the flames of her fire, and mine.

If you have the fire, nothing, nothing, nothing, can douse the flame. Once again, my whole being is aflame with joy.

Life rises anew in the wisps of smoke.

Donor can you feel the warmth on my hands? Karyn has reached the 12th day of rehab. More days of rehab completed than waiting.

This Monday, Karyn has an esophageal manometry test. The esophageal motility test identifies problems with movement and pressure in the esophagus. The esophagus is the food pipe leading from the mouth to the stomach. Manometry measures the strength and muscle coordination of your esophagus when you swallow. A small catheter tube is passed through the nose, along the back of the throat, down the esophagus, and into the stomach.

Lung transplant patients have a high incidence of gastric reflux disease, (GERD), which puts them at risk for aspiration events in which reflux travels into your lungs, sounding the immune system's alarms. Reflux may contribute to the rejection of your lungs, by injuring them when it's inhaled. Hopefully, Karyn will do well and not need the dreaded stomach wrap. 'Cause she promised the doctors she would not do the wrap.

The stomach is wrapped where it meets the esophagus, so you can no longer throw up and aspirate into your lungs. Karyn's stomach is as small as her heart is big, and too many people have had difficulties with the wrap, so I will pray that the test results show no need for the wrap. One of my friends said he will pray as well. His prayers are always the same. In the morning, his prayer is "Whatever" and his evening prayer, "Oh Well."

I know Karyn is fragile and a softy. She is tough and kick-ass. We can deal with the wrap.

The stomach tests. Whatever. Oh well.

Somehow I don't get bogged down in the details, never, ever forgetting we are alive, thanks to your gift, and living it. Fire breathers we all are.

Talk to you soon,

Richard

Monday June 29, 2009

The Other Side

Dear Donor,

Wishing my wife good prayers and good luck from the pit of my stomach.

The next test is the swallowing test. Foods of different consistencies are stained with a green dye so the technician can watch the food pass from the mouth into the esophagus, to see where it may be held up and to make sure it does not enter the larynx.

Normal swallowing achieves two goals: transporting food from the mouth to the stomach and protecting the airway. During the oral phase, food is chewed, mixed with saliva, and pushed to the back of the mouth. This part of swallowing is voluntary. Once the food enters the pharynx, swallowing becomes involuntary, stimulated by reflexes. Normal swallowing at this point propels the food downward towards the esophagus, and prevents food from going up behind the nose or into the lungs. If food enters the airway and goes into the lungs, this is called "aspiration" and may result in pneumonia or other serious illness and rejection. Once the food is in the esophagus, it is propelled downwards to the stomach.

We are 12 hours into the tests and if the future is like the past, Karyn will knock 'em dead again. As the warm and friendly clinician stated, most transplant patients would pay top dollar for Karyn's test numbers. The swallow test was great and so far the reflux test is just an irritating little tube down the throat.

Karyn's days are winding down here in North Carolina, and she is winding up.

The weekend was restful, and at one time, I noticed a color I had not seen in many years. It was pink, not in what Karyn was wearing, but in her cheeks. It was the most beautiful shade of pink, so becoming and radiated the essence of health. So when you see the color pink, think of Karyn and remember how hard she has worked to wear this color.

Nine days of rehab left, her numbers are good, and looking forward to getting this show on the road.

In the pink,

Richard

Airhead, Things
Better Left Unsaid
The Other Side

Tuesday June 30, 2009

Thinking back to this afternoon at the DUKE Center for Living, one man poked jabs at several older men; that he should be transplanted before them, that it does not make a difference what stage their disease was, that they had lived their lives and it was now the younger man's turn. Another man emphatically jumped in "That LAM is not a known, and that all persons with pulmonary fibrosis should always go first." "LAM is a nothing." LAM to the back-of-the-bus.

LAM is nothing. Nothing. I thought about what this word meant, what it really meant to be nothing. To be of no import. No value. It was one of those moments when I felt I had never heard the word before, and I could not believe it means what it means. I thought how did this word come to mean that? Nothing. A common word you could use for anything. "Nothing's wrong." The way he used it, it sounded final, like a verdict. "LAM is a nothing", he repeated. Better not check my BP after that conversation.

I, the mouth, once felt not-so-long-ago, that those with chronic obstructive pulmonary disease (COPD), who had smoked up their lungs should go to the back of the bus, or even off the bus. Their disease was self-inflicted nothing. Words that I want to vacuum back, flew out of my mouth. COPD is nothing. I could not think of any meaning of the word idiot that did not apply to me.

I have heard in other conversations that LAM (or fill in the disease) is a gift. LAM is not a gift, and yes Karyn has changed for the better because of it, but that does not make it a gift. If it does, I am sure she would like to return it. Anyone else want to queue up in this line?

Whatever disease anyone has at The Center for Living, it wreaks havoc on those who have it and the lives of all those people who care about them. If only I had cystic fibrosis instead of LAM. If only I had pulmonary fibrosis instead of LAM. One disease over another is not something to be sought; it is never the lesser of evils. Any long-term and debilitating disease sucks. No lung disease is nothing.

It does not matter how grave things are for you, there is always someone worse, but it does not matter because your pain and suffering is your own, and that is enough. Those of us who opened our mouth and felt age should trump lung scores. Those of us who felt one disease is worse than another, and me, the one who felt that those-who-smoked-up-their-lungs should get off the bus. I know we have all opened our mouths and said something we were sorry for later. I know what it is like to make an off-handed remark only to later realize the insensitive impact my words can bestow upon others. God do I know this. Words have meanings and they have consequences.

We all suffer, we all experience things differently and trading one horrible disease for another does not solve any problems. Each disease knows no mercy. All of us in the disease world, I know now; are all connected—you can no more separate one life from another than you can separate a breeze from the wind.

My mom wisely said to me, and I am sure more than I can count, "It is better to be silent and have people think you are stupid, then open your mouth and eliminate all doubt." I tell myself it was fear ignorance that my wife would not be transplanted at University of Colorado Hospital that brought me to this COPD position. I am sure it was fear at DUKE for the younger man and husband to speak of age and disease "superiority." What were they or I thinking? Or were we even thinking? Sometimes the price of our words is more than we can afford.

143

You know, if being on oxygen was so much fun, dealers would be selling it on the black market. I know I'd much prefer a cold to a brain tumor or Alzheimer's, but I guess it really does not matter, like any one of us dealing with a disease had a menu in front of us and decided on the LAM very rare, over the equally delectable Cystic Fibrosis, the scrumptious Pulmonary Fibrosis, or the very well-done COPD.

I know now it is silly to compare or rank diseases. I would say that CF, LAM, COPD or PF, is neither the greater nor the lesser evil. After all how can any of us gauge another person's suffering? There is no one-upmanship in suffering. When people suffer, and are afraid we say all kinds of insensitive things. At essence, we are all simple human beings who are hurt and scared.

My Grandpa Harmon said it best; always walk a mile in someone else's shoes before you wish to own them.

There's No Place Like Hope
The Other Side

I am not surprised how well Karyn has done post-transplant. Maybe some of the evaluating DUKE psychologists are surprised, as prescribed Xanax use pre-transplant listing was a major issue. But Karyn was only on Xanax as prescribed by her local doctor to reduce the anxiety of not-being-able-to-breathe. Who would not be anxious when you cannot catch your breath? Anyone? Ever been in the ocean and forced under by one large wave after another and not able to catch your breath? It's an awful, awful feeling. With LAM, you always have that fear; it is always with you, that you can't get another breath and come up with air.

The fear of some on the transplant team was that Karyn would wither under the pressures of post-rehab. Succumb to the anxiety and fall apart. A transplant wasted. Those on the team were in error; they simply did not know Karyn. I know Karyn and Karyn is Hope.

Who knows what we are really capable of? Who knows what Karyn is really capable of? The Xanaxers were wrong. No one can teach you how to be you. No one can teach me how to be me. No one could tell Karyn how far she could go or not go. No one could tell Karyn how much she could take. No one could tell Karyn when enough was enough because no one really knew other than Karyn, and Karyn had to learn it herself.

Before Karyn was diagnosed with LAM, I was sure there were certain problems that were just too big for her, or us. But now I know better. I

145

know that each of us can alter virtually anything that comes our way. All of us are capable of amazing things if we just set our own compass to it.

Karyn saw hope. Karyn saw the light in the darkness of the dark. She had strength even in her physical weakness. She found grace.

Without hope, I could not find a foothold in life. There is nothing healthy that can live in this world without hope. Hope is all we have or need. Sometimes hope is all that keeps me going from one moment to the next. It's okay to have doubts, even as I hope.

LAM can't kill my hope. There is not a surgeon alive who can cut it out. With hope, I can deal with incredible hardships and keep going. Hope always reminds me that my heart is eavesdropping on my brain, that my heart pumps for my mind to believe in healing, and then for my body to reach it. Hope came from my sister LAMMIES and the LAM Foundation—they were my big bouncy house. No matter how hard I hit the wall, they cushioned my falls.

Hope is the thread that weaves its way through my body, that connects my heart to my brain. My body listens to the signals of my spirit. God gave me hope when God gave me life. When I was born, I hoped to be picked up, changed, fed and coddled. What I hope for will change a thousand times throughout my life, but with the very last breath I draw, I will be hoping. I have faith in faith and I have hope in hope itself.

With Hope, I tap into a power beyond myself. Hope can change the way I see and hear. Hope is what pushes me to the next step. Hope is what keeps me moving forward. Hope is its own reward.

I have little pet names for those in rehab with Karyn. There is Coach, Sarge, Deer-In-The-Headlights, The Little Engine that Could, the Professor, the Beacon and Ever-ready. Karyn, the Cheerleader, always with a smile, always bringing hope, and sharing hope. Hope and optimism waft off her like a strong scent. I see Karyn with her lung torch held high in the air, The Statue of Hope. Her LAM was never contagious, but her hope certainly is. Can you feel the heat from her torch?

Hope is the small voice that God speaks to my heart, instead of my head. Hope is a well, which I always drink from and my well is very deep. Hope allowed me to drink from the well when my body was too weak and my breath too thin. Hope gave me that extra-added little ooomph to heal. Hope is breath for my soul.

I remember when I was little reading and re-reading the Little Engine that Could. Even the little engine was allowed to say, I think I can, I think I can. It was Hope that can make it and hope keeps me chugging along. The Little Engine is the Center for Living exercise rehab for my body and Hope is exercise for my soul.

I keep hope brightly lit so everyone else can see it.

I remember when I was young, well maybe not that young and reading Emily Dickinson "Hope is the thing with feathers that perches in the soul, and sings the tune without the words and never stops at all."

The hope Karyn has and shares costs nothing. Maybe Karyn should charge a fee for hope so we would have a better sense of its value. Step right up, ladies and gentlemen, Hope for sale. The line forms to the right, no pushing. But of course no one could afford it, for the value of hope, like the taste of breath, is priceless.

Dear Donor,

Karyn will have her GJ tube removed on Thursday. It is an in-hospital procedure. She will not be sedated and when she awakens, the tube will be gone. A five minute procedure and the tube contorting Karyn's stomach will be gone. The GJ tube would get mucked up, and a caffeinated beverage is used to clean it. I shall remember the time I used regular Coke, straight from the refrigerator and sent milk-shake headache shivers into Karyn and rocketed her diabetes numbers into the stratosphere. To clean the GJ tube, Coke, lukewarm and diet. Repeat after me, lukewarm and diet. Clinic day is tomorrow, and blood draws, chest x-rays, the evil ABG's, PFT's, and a meet with the doctor.

Each and every day is a gift, and I am feeling today that some presents are just better than others.

My heart goes out to you, and I hope your family is healing,

Richard

Dorothy, with apologies. Now I am going to click my heels together and say, "There's no place like Hope. There's no place like Hope. There's no place like hope."

Things always change which, for me, means that there's always hope and I breathe in hope, and take very deep breaths.

No pushing. Stay in line. We'll be handing out numbers. The line forms to the right. Hope. Catch it.

Never stop hoping.

Heroes No Longer Fly Through the Air
The Other Side

Monday July 6, 2009

When I was a boy, I thought that strong meant having big muscles and great physical power. But the longer I live, the more I realize that real strength has much more to do with what is not seen, has more to do with one's own inertia, with one's will to come to terms with the unknown paths of LAM and of lung disease.

Most of my childhood heroes wore capes, flew through the air, and picked up buildings with one arm. They were spectacular and got a lot of attention, but over time, my heroes changed, so that now I can honestly say that those who deal with LAM, with lung disease, with the gauntlet of transplant, are my real heroes.

I think as Americans our hero stories are of individuals who overcome adversity. The determination and focus of the pilot who lands the plane without engines, or the hiker that survives a fall and hobbles out of the wilderness with a shattered leg is like a Lammie's or Lungie's journey through loss and transplant.

You take it one step at a time, focus on just getting through the wilderness of the day, the week, the next set-back. But, for Karyn and the others transplanted, the story does not end there. They are never out of the woods. They are caught in a snare that they can't extract themselves out of.

I no longer believe that heroes are extraordinary people. I believe they are everyday people like Karyn, and others in her class at the Center for Living,

Gene, John, and Paul. They are just ordinary people in extraordinary circumstances. These are my heroes, for they have learned to love their journey through the wilderness, and not just the destination.

Dear Donor,

Having LAM and a lung transplant means that each day I live is a mini-survival story

We walk a hard road. Every Lammie and Lungie clears the roads for each of us, and hopefully, relieving some of our own potholes. The clock never truly stops, even when things are going well. It's always there ticking in the background. You have to have it in you to keep going, for however long, to whatever place, taking one step at a time. I live that life with joy; that is my victory and hopefully, that may very well be a gift to others.

Each day I live, I honor you, donor, my special hero, who-has-no-name. You didn't fly through the air, but you gave me air. You didn't lift any building with one arm, but you lifted me up with your two lungs.

You were only one person in the whole wide world, but to me, you are my whole world, who selflessly saved my life.

The road ahead is not easy for any of us, but all of us ordinary people will live it to our best.

Karyn

With All My Breath
Both Sides

Karyn's lung collapsed the first time in 1980 and again with her pregnancy in 1981. Karyn had an angeiomyolopoma removed from her kidney in 1991. In 1999, diagnosed with LAM, and now sucking air, not able to catch her breath, and no longer even able to keep up with herself.

I would watch Karyn breathe; looking like a fish out of water, not able to get enough air, even with supplemental oxygen. At night, while she slept, I would place both my hands on her back, wishing, praying, for my own lungs, my own oxygen, to somehow magically flow from my body into her lungs, and make her whole. Wishing that she could take the breath from my own lungs, and be able to hike, and dance, and play once again.

This morning I pass so many people busy with the thoughts of the coming day, not aware of how wonderful it is just to breathe in and out. Most do not care enough for air. The average person inhales about 26,000 times a day, taking in about 14,000 liters, or about 150 bathtubs' worth of air. After all, air is not diamonds or gold, fine wine or a new car, or fashionable attire or a painting, something you can admire and hang on the wall.

When breathing for Karyn could no longer be taken for granted, when just walking across a room or up the dreaded stairs became a high act of determination, Karyn saw wonder in breathing, and caring for air; she came to care more for the things air has to do with. People and objects changed for her, came closer, became very dear. When she could no longer take in enough air, she became quietly more real to herself than in the

151

Zion and Disco years, when the taking in of air, was a simple, hardly-to-be-thought-of-fact.

Today, Karyn is breathing air right in front of my face. She sits still as her lung pressure brings air in, and it goes into her nostrils and mouth, the back of her throat and into her lungs and belly. The air she is breathing, I am breathing. We are breathing it together. We are sharing the same air. Those trees outside our room are also breathing, and making our breaths possible. Her breath is like a river of air, meandering in and out of her body, quenching my thirst for her.

Dear Donor,

It's me Karyn. Or should I say, It's you.

I used to take some things for granted, like the love of my husband and my children, the sun rising tomorrow, and the breathing of fresh air from my lungs. But no more. I remember Richard trying so very hard at night while he thought I was sleeping, to pour his breath into me through his fingers. When something is taken from you, when I could no later count on my next breath, it makes me realize what the gift of your lungs granted me.

Too many people take breaths but do not give breaths. God knows, I so feel your breath, donor, and am thoroughly impressed.

On our walk tonight around the Residence Inn this evening, the air whispered and I looked skyward at the moon. It seemed so very far away and yet close enough for me to touch. Man in the moon, can you feel my breath?

I took a deep breath as we strolled around the Residence Inn, enjoying the smell after rain; sometimes just a simple smell can make me happy. Did you like the smell of the world after a cleansing rain?

Breathing the air you gave me is nothing less than a particle of grace.

No longer taking things for granted.

Thank you Donor, and thank you God.

With you,

Karyn

Dear Donor,

I remember when Karyn could not take in enough air, like her lungs had pinhole leaks. Last night, we walked our evening mosey around the parking lot of the Residence Inn, doing the loop again and again and again. Our hands come easily together and the stars seemed to pulse with brightening light, and I felt the slow breathing of the earth beneath us. Is that you?

I inhale, exhale, look up at the sky seeing my lucky star, and at Karyn, who had once again handed me her heart.

Karyn is now asleep and I stare. She draws in air, a long slow draft of it, and as she slowly releases it, her breathing falls into the easy rhythms of sleep. The breath that escapes from Karyn is dazzled, and I breathe it in, with a sigh. Donor, I can taste your breath and I am sighing.

After all these years. Karyn still takes my breath away.

The gift of breathing you granted us. I will pass it on,

Richard

THURSDAY JULY 2, 2009

Dear Donor,

The GJ tube is removed. Five minutes and the tube contorting Karyn's stomach is gone. Clinic day is tomorrow. Karyn aced both her swallowing and reflux tests and the dreaded stomach wrap is not needed. I wonder had she failed the tests and if a wrap would have been needed. With Karyn not wanting the wrap, would the doctors have won that argument? This boxer in my string would have won this bout, "stomach down." I bet all of the staff would have needed Xanax after that battle.

Sunday July 10, 2009

Our 38th anniversary and we celebrate with another couple, Gene and Malinda Holley, from our rehab class. Karyn bought a pedometer and set a goal of 10,000 steps in a day, about 5 miles. (On Wednesday, she reached her goal).

As we walked around the Residence Inn this evening as the sun was slowly setting, and a welcome motion of air produced a slight cooling breeze whistling through the foliage of the nearby trees, a son of a fellow lung transplant said it best, Karyn looks vibrant.

Karyn's brown eyes twinkled and she gave me a sly smile. Her eyes were dreamy and the smile that slightly parted her lips was pure and sincere. Her breath so very warm in my ear. Pulsating with life, the word vibrant ringing in my head like a bell, shining and pure. I could hear it pealing with its true meaning, and I said, as if I had just realized it, that Karyn is vibrant.

The next morning we visited a post-lung transplant and fellow rehabber who has been in the hospital over 6 weeks. Karyn's grace and vibrancy touched him as well.

Two more rehab sessions Monday and Tuesday and clinic on Wednesday.

Donor, thanks for watching over us.

Richard

The Center for Living, Last Days
The Other Side

Monday July 13, 2009

Dear Donor,

Like High School's finale before graduation, the last bells are tolling. Karyn grabs phone numbers, addresses, and e-mail addresses. The electronic ways replacing the yearbook. That same excitement of the final week before you make your own way in the world. Karyn is graduating DUKE.

We will always remember the blessings that were bestowed. We will always remember that riches are not retained until returned.

We've been through much and will go through much more. Traveling 2gether is more fun, whatever life and love may have in store; 2 is always preferable to one. Karyn's graduation becomes my pleasure; her happiness is mine, a double treasure. No one could be more blessed than I with her. When you have seen how fragile life truly is, you are indeed blessed.

Love's a very generous reward. One of us is the tune and one of us the chord. The music in my heart is very lovely as the melody plays on.

For every ending there is a new beginning. For every memory, there is a dream ahead, whisking Karyn to the corners of her smiles.

The harmonies of the song play, of pride and sadness, of those who are here and those no longer with us, the dawn and sunset of new and the old, the bittersweet goodbyes of looking forward.

Dearest Karyn, I am so very proud because I am a part of everything you do. I want a bumper sticker on my car that reads, Proud husband of an honor student at the DUKE Center for Living.

It is time to say how much in love I am with you. How many years ago did you write in my yearbook, and I in yours? The melody plays on. How sweet the rhythms have become.

This morning Tracie, our post-transplant coordinator, told Karyn she is good to go after completing her final two sessions, today and tomorrow, and labs on Wednesday. Karyn will leave DUKE this Saturday as the journey moves back to Colorado.

2 Good
2 Be
4 Gotten

God, give me these moments, please, forever. Replicate it for me, on demand. The gift of memory; now that's a true gift.

With love,

Richard

Tuesday July 14, 2009

Dear Donor,

Karyn is at rehab now, her last day. The number is zero. Did I say zero has no meaning? There is much meaning in today.

Karyn will do her final 6 minute walk. How far will she walk? Yesterday she walked more laps than ever before for the 20 minute walk. Yesterday, she walked at rehab and around the Residence Inn, putting in almost 2 miles.

At rehab today I watch Karyn say farewell knowing that the special attachments and bonds will never be broken. Karyn will continue to feel that special bond though words may not be spoken. It's not goodbye but farewell. We'll see you again my friends. Your friendship means a lot to me, and it will never end.

Donor, thank you for bringing back my wife,

Richard

THIS AIN'T BASEBALL
BOTH SIDES

Dear Donor,

(A League of Their Own, as spoken by Tom Hanks) "Are you Crying? Are you crying? Are you crying? There's no crying! There's no crying in baseball!" But I can tell you there's crying in LAM, Lung Disease, Transplant, ICU.

I was not a crier for a very long time. With Karyn's LAM illness, the ups-and-downs of the roller coaster world of pre—and post-transplant, I have become a crier and have turned on those emotional faucets, which were rusty from disuse. People become more emotional, it is said, when they take drugs. Maybe I just caught that drug of emotion.

I have found tears I never knew I had. When a lung patient stayed in the hospital for over two months, when another Lungie suffered a horrific life-threatening setback. When one of our rehab friends suffered on the brink, I cried. The overwhelming sadness was like the breaking of a dam, a tidal wave of tears. It's like I tapped into a well, deep inside my heart where it is breaking. The harder I tried not to cry, the harder I cried. Wet cheeks kept my heart from drying up inside. Guys, life throws you a lot of curveballs, but this ain't baseball.

When Karyn suffered her stroke, tears were exclamation points to what I felt. Tears showed me the rawness of my feelings, sometimes the sad, but also the frustration, delight, anger, love, and joy. Gigantic drums of tears stockpiled finally let loose, the tears ran silently down my face. I cried because my heart knew I had so much more to learn. Is it true the more you cry now, the less you cry later? Were there a certain amount of tears that needed to be cried out? Will the tears ever go away?

I cried when Karyn could barely breathe before transplant and was so very exhausted from literally doing nothing. When she did not know she had been transplanted, and could again breathe on room air, I suffered a pulsing wave of tears upon tears. My tears flowing freely like the rain. It amazed me how strong my heart could be, even when it was breaking.

I am no longer afraid of tears. I know now that each drop has so much compassion and love in it and so I let the tears flow easily and wear the tear stains proudly. Tears are my badge of despair and heartache and compassion. Tears, like grief, reveals myself to me.

I found that crying is a strange phenomenon, because it does not occur when and where I thought it would happen. When I heard from doctors about the stroke-like episode setback for Karyn, the strength that I used to keep a positive front fended off the tears. After visiting with Karyn in writhing pain, and unable to move her left side, I picked up dinner from a restaurant and glanced at a couple sharing a meal; the idea of eating normally was something that literally tore me apart, and caused me to burst into a puddle of tears. I felt the sting of those tears and a sensation of pain so deep that I could barely breathe.

When it's going well, it's everywhere: in the program on TV, the song on the radio, the settings at a dinner table. And when it's all going badly, it's in all the same places. In the end, it's not the changes that break your heart; it's that tug of familiarity.

God gave me tear ducts, and God wanted me to cry. I know that tears are God's way of cleansing and washing away. Sometimes tears wash away a speck of dirt in my eye and sometimes they wash away a bit of something in my heart and mind. People talk about crying from happiness and it sounds stupid, crying from happiness. I never knew what it meant. It's not really happiness that makes the tears, it's everything at once, everything that's good and sad and wonderful all at once, except the things that are wonderful mean so much more than the sad things. So much more.

A woman I had been sitting with for many days in ICU cried often. Her husband of so many years had taken ill very quickly and as he passed away, she cried. Her tears saturating the tissues, shoulders heaving with every wracking sob. I will never forget her words as she cried and cried on my shoulder, she told me that she had read it somewhere and as a crier, kept it close to her heart. "If I could have been any part of my husband, I would be his tear. Conceived in his heart, born in his eyes, alive on his cheek, and died on his lips." Tears are indeed a blessing, as I cried and handed her a tissue. Tears are healing, and they are loving. "I'll go get us another box of tissues."

In the ICU waiting room, I thought how sad it must be when someone is ill or dying, and no one cries for them. There are no tears to mark the depth of love. How sad it was when a person told me "Don't cry," after Karyn had her episode. Who are they to say crying is bad?

Dear Donor,

Just a brief note before I go to bed. Karyn and I walked again this evening, the hardest walk-to-date, much of it uphill, and steep, a total of over 5 miles. Several stops along the way as her O2 level dipped into the 80's. The oxygen level needs to be over 90. I can hear the cry from the old TV show E.R. yelling out "Pulse-Ox"!

As we walked, dusk was turning to nightfall. The sky was brilliant with colors. Golds and yellows and blues morphing into lavenders. I glanced away for a moment, and the lavender was on fire, now a flaming red. Then ever-so-quickly the red was gone and the clouds burned fiery orange. The colors so bright remind me of not-too-long-ago Karyn's facial "colors" were but a stark metal green and gray. Now like the sky at sunset, her colors are a rosy palette, so bright and her glow a-flame.

Blood test this week showed very high levels of cyclosporine. The cyclosporine was at 472, and should be no more than the normal 350. Cyclosporine in too-high a dose can be toxic. This high level may explain

Karyn's cold hands and feet, her dizziness, light-headedness, and low blood pressure. Maybe even her oxygen drop into the 80's. I am glad Karyn will return to DUKE next week for her regular tests and bronch.

As we turned towards home last night, lightning lit up the skies. I told Karyn it was God taking her picture with an old Eastman Kodak, and the flashbulbs going off. I am sure God will show you her photo.

I see the new beginnings and hurry home from the office. Karyn, to me, is just like getting a new puppy. Remember running home from school or work to be with your new pooch? Puppy love surely is great. Being married for almost 40 years, and in puppy love?

Arf.

In my thoughts,

Richard

A Negative is a Positive—On
Borrowed Time, On the Clock
The Other Side

The bronchoscopy showed acute rejection, and Karyn is in the midst of fighting off A-1 mild rejection. Two out of three lung transplant patients will have acute rejection. Why couldn't Karyn be the third?

Rejection is very common, as the immune system recognizes the donor lung tissue as foreign material that must be destroyed. Thinking it is doing its duty, the body sends its cellular troops to attack the infidel. To outflank this problem, doctors suppress the patient's immune system with medicines that trick Karyn's body into thinking the new lungs are hers. These same medicines can make Karyn susceptible to ordinary infections that otherwise she would be capable of battling.

It is a delicate tightrope act between suppressing the immune system so that the new lungs can graft within the new body and yet allow the immune system to function well enough to avoid being overwhelmed with routine bacteria or viruses. The operative word is delicate.

The immune response to the transplanted organ protects the body from potentially harmful substances (antigens) such as microorganisms, toxins and cancer cells. No two people except identical twins have identical tissue antigens. Without immunosuppressant drugs, organ transplantation would almost always cause an immune response against the foreign tissue (rejection), which would result in the destruction of the transplant. The immunosuppressive drugs are used to keep this response in check, but often the body's impulse to defend itself simply takes over.

Acute rejection is injury to the organ caused by the T-lymphocytes. These cells were seen during Karyn's bronch and found with the biopsy of the lung. Biopsies of the lung are done at regular intervals to check for presence of rejection, and are done at one month, three months, six months, nine months and twelve months. The lungs then are biopsied every 12 months in absence of any problem.

Biopsies are done through a lighted tube, a bronchoscope, that is inserted through the nose or throat and into the lungs. The throat is sprayed with a numbing medication, and the bronchoscope is inserted. Most patients are put under. This procedure is uncomfortable, and your throat lets you know about this, as coughing spells are normal. The tissue is examined and if there is the presence of rejection and infection, Karyn is notified immediately.

Rejection usually but not always occurs in the first month or the first year after transplant. Karyn's rejection, A1, which is minimal acute rejection, is the mildest rejection. Karyn had shown symptoms of A1 rejection—tightness in her chest and a recent persistent cough. She received home infusions of antibiotics and steroids administered by Apria Home Healthcare for three days. Her prednisone level was increased from 20mg per day to about 500mg through the butterfly IV in an hour. After the infusion period, she will take 60mg by pill and then taper off each day by 5mg, until back to 20mg. Steroids! Guess who will be tip-toeing around the house?

Dear Donor,

Just to let you know, a little bout of acute rejection but don't worry. Nothing stops the-little-engine-that-could Karyn. For the last three days of IV steroid infusions I tell myself there is nothing to be gained by worrying between then and now, and yet I still worried. Karyn walked almost fifteen miles in those three days. Today, she babysat Avah and took the little one to a not-so-nearby park to swing and play. One thing I don't worry about is that my wife does not have acute rejection to being positive. If there was a blood test for optimists, she would test positive. And the pessimists and their blood test would show up as "B negative." Sorry for that bad joke.

When I cough, I do not worry. Karyn asks me "Am I all right?" and I answer yes. I do not worry. When Karyn coughs, once, twice, three times, and I ask, "Are you okay?" and Karyn says, "I am fine." I worry. Every ache and pain of hers makes me wonder if the LAM is coming back, or if your lungs are being called back to you. LAM can come back but in all likelihood, rejection will take her life, not the LAM. Rejection affects the entire body. As you know a transplant is the last resort of last resorts.

Life death life death life death. The rhythm of life going back and forth like a metronome. Karyn's transplant day of pills and shots starts at 7:00 AM and ends at 10:00 PM. If you are tired, too bad—you need to get up, and be up. For the rest of her life, Karyn's transplant day schedule must be met. There are no days off. There is no retirement. You cut out the LAM with your lungs, but LAM is a weed that can grow back.

As a husband, I call tell you honestly there are times, sometimes even long stretches where I forget my wife has LAM and your lungs, and just see Karyn as my wife, as a woman. Of course, those long stretches—and by long, I mean hours or days, at the most—do end and I am left marveling at her, and how she is not supposed to be around right now either, and then I look forward to forgetting again.

You know this, but many people do not, that with a transplant you are trading one chronic disease for another chronic disease. The LAM is not gone. The LAM can come back. The battle to keep your lungs from being attacked by aliens is always on. Karyn has not been cured. What all this is about is buying time. Transplant is trading one set of problems for a hopefully more manageable set.

The transplant survival rate at the end of 1 year is 85%, at 3 years 76% and at 5 years, 60%. Unfortunately 40 per cent of recipients die within five years of transplant. When you get a transplant, you set the clock. No offense, but at some point, the immune systems registers that the transplanted organ is foreign material. Is it because every time Karyn breathes in air, her lungs are at risk? No other organ transplant is exposed like your lungs.

Karyn avoids cigarette smoke, estrogen-containing medications, and working in the soil, with its germy spores. She sits in the back of rooms so that anyone coughing; coughs forward. She wears a mask on an airplane as air is re-circulated. Karyn either avoids buffets or has to be first in line. When she coughs or is tired or her color is not pink, I worry, is she all right?

I worry about the Dark Side, Bronchiolitis Obliterans Syndrome (BOS), chronic rejection. This is the nasty progressive deterioration of the function of your lungs. Unlike acute rejection, BOS does not respond to currently available medical treatment. BOS maybe related to repeated infections or rejection episodes. Sadly, BOS is common and the most common cause of transplant death. BOS can be treated, not cured, and many people live with it, for many years. Unfortunately, at the present, immunosuppressant drugs and the balancing act is more an art than a science, with too many transplanted succumbing to rejection or infection.

DUKE is studying BOS. I am hopeful that a cure will be found. Like everything, it takes money to study this awful disease. As my mom says, it should be as easy to make it as it is to spend it.

I hear no coughing from Karyn and I am going to go to sleep.

I will keep you posted,

Richard

Dear Donor,

I am three months out, as you know, and I am on heavy doses of steroids to get rid of some mild rejection of your lungs. Don't take it personally; these things happen. My body is a war zone. I take one pill to fight rejection and my kidneys go haywire. I take pills to fight off rejection and my weakened body suffers acute rejection.

I am surviving LAM and your lung transplant. I guess that changes the noun to a verb. It is something I am doing, not what I am.

I am still sick after transplant, but it is a different kind of sick. There are challenges for me for the remainder of my life. Rejection is always around the corner. It is the mask of death peeking through the curtains. There will never fully be any time of rest. What I have done, as you know, is merely postpone the inevitable. I cling to the time I have been granted to learn the true meanings of life as I struggle with knowledge of my mortality, and I am glad your lungs are along for the ride.

Sometimes I feel like I am always looking over my shoulder and will never truly feel safe again. Never feel safe again; now that's a scary thought. There is no doctor at DUKE or at home whose role is to make me safe. They are there to fix me when things go awry. Can I ever feel safe in any part of my life? Am I supposed to?

Anything can happen when you step out the front door, and I guess you know that (although you have not told me what happened to you). A tree hit by lightning crashing into me. That darn bus.

But that's life. Dare to love and you risk rejection and a broken heart. Dare to speak out and you risk condemnation. Apply for that new job and you risk rejection. Our daily lives are full of risk and rejection. But without risk there is no more to be gained than lost.

Normal and safe is an illusion. Sometimes I think the illusion of safety, the illusion of unlimited time unfolding into the future, of "later," and "someday" is something we humans maintain as we need it. But my life is an adventure, meant to be lived. Full of ups and downs, risks and rewards, triumphs and defeats. Never safety. Not true safety. Like normal, safety is an illusion. The illusion of unlimited time of Later and Someday is just that, an illusion.

Feeling safe is forgetting about it, so easy, and still too hard, to ever feel safe. Life isn't an illusion that's meant to be safe. And I don't think it's meant to be.

Will I ever see myself the way I used to? I do not think so. Settling into the new normal takes a long time. It is like a series of earthquakes and aftershocks. Just when I am getting comfortable along comes another reminder. Do not get me wrong, I am always a glass full kind of person, so it's not like I dwell on my LAM and your lung transplant all the time. But it is always there, lurking around like a bad dog, waiting to bite me when I least expect it—like vomiting and aspirating into your lungs and almost immediately getting pneumonia or walking in the neighborhood and picking up aspergillis from someone just mowing their lawn and getting acute rejection.

I can get LAM's sinister sister; one can get LAM and it can come back. The lungs can be rejected. I am paroled but not free.

Is the bark worse than the bite? I drift back to the week of evaluations at DUKE in February before my transplant, and the gauntlet of tests: the blood draws, the pulmonary function tests, the echocardiogram, the heart catheterization, the chest CT scans, the gastric pH test, and the esophageal manometry test. Phew. I remember the six minute walk at the Center for Living and struggling to pass the 1000 feet barrier requirement.

I can hear the words of one of the thoracic surgeons, "You don't want a transplant. No one does. If you think you have trouble breathing now, it will be much worse after we cut through your intercostal muscles. You'll be in such pain and misery, many days you will regret you had this operation."

"If you think you can walk in here and get new lungs, and you'll be fine, you will not. You will be miserable. For the rest of your life, you must take strong drugs to prevent rejection of foreign tissue that will weaken your whole body and make you more susceptible to diseases you would never have gotten otherwise." Like many kinds of cancer and diabetes. The drugs induce diabetes in about half of transplant patients (you can see me and I am raising my hand as one of them). "Quality of life? You think it will be better after transplant—it will be worse because you will be so miserable."

And I asked, "What's the alternative if I do not get a transplant?"

The answer, "We all die."

The most important lesson of all doctor, "We all die," is the pain will pass. And almost all of the time, it's worth it. It's the price I pay to stay in the game.

Some days I play the LAM or Lung Transplant card. Some days I just keep it in my pocket. I carry the label, whether it be a designer label or one just off the rack. But I do not want to be remembered only for the LAM and the Lung Transplant. I was not that before and am more than that after. I keep thinking about it and thinking about it and I want to shout it out, but if I did, then I would be bringing up the LAM and transplant thing—I suspect I am still remembered as LAM girl, as Lung Transplant Lady. I just try to remind myself, to remember what I believe they would want to remember.

LAM and your transplant have given me time, time to love, time to laugh, time to feel the love around me, and tell them that I love them. As life will someday come to a close (Yes doctor, we all die) I can tell you all, that the time was well spent.

Hopeful for future bronchs being negative, which is positive.

Karyn

The Abbreviation of Genuine is Gene
On Both Sides

Karyn and I had traveled the farthest distance to come to Duke, and thankfully, we met Gene and Malinda Holley the first week we were ensconced at the Residence Inn. The Lungies here and at DUKE became our family.

Gene Holley had been hospitalized in 1993 with an upper respiratory infection. Five years later, he came down with pneumonia and when he left the hospital he was on supplemental oxygen 24/7. Gene was diagnosed with COPD and his lung capacity was down to only 17%—the road from their home in Cashiers in the Blue Ridge to Durham in August of 2008 led Gene to run the gauntlet of tests at DUKE for admittance to the DUKE Lung Transplant Program.

Gene laughed, which he did a lot, about how he had been poked, prodded and violated in every orifice of his body. Before his next appointment three months later, He was given a laundry list of things to get done; the top of the list was to lose 25 to 30 pounds. Gene attacked the lost weight with the tenacity of a D-1 football coach running fall camp two-a-days. At the beginning of March, Gene was admitted to the rehab program, Karyn's boot camp class at the DUKE Center for Living.

Gene always had a sparkle in his eye, a beaming smile on his face which, when you suck air like a beached trout on a river bank, while lugging an oxygen "golf cart" behind you, is anything but easy. Gene's sparkling eyes were always so clear, so sincere. He was always encouraging me and everyone else, his eyes twinkling like the stars in the heavens and his smile brighter than the sun. "The more you do on this side, the easier it will be on the other side." Gently prodding, never mad or tired, The Coach, coaxing everyone in our rehab program to do just a little bit more, and then to do some more. He was like my granddaughter, Avah, on the swings. "More." "Higher." "More." The Coach made everyone feel better, more relaxed, and our spirits, both patient and care-giver, uplifted to the heavens. "Higher." Gene brought air to the room. COPD surely is not infectious, but Gene's spirit was contagious. Gene was a special person who radiated a natural magnetic field, who everyone is drawn to, who everyone is dazzled by.

We celebrated our anniversary with Gene and his wife, and a few weeks later at the end of July, Gene was transplanted, two months after Karyn. Gene is the only patient I know who walked under his own power from the surgery clean room to his cubicle in ICU. Four days out in step-down, and the physical therapist was telling him to slow down on his walks around the hallways, as what was called for was endurance not speed. Day four and he walked a mile. Discussion was underway to send Gene home. On Saturday, a week out, Gene called Malinda at 6 o'clock in the morning, asking when she was coming to take him home. He then walked the halls and very un-like Gene, prayed aloud with another man. The

Coach magically and miraculously inspired all he met. The gift he had, he shared.

Two short hours later Gene went into full cardiac arrest, his brain oxygen-deprived. How could this have happened? The doctors hedged, used lots of big words, and after trying everything the end tolled on the 14th day.

Gene relished every breath he took for those seven days. He received the ultimate gift and was so very, very thankful for it. His new motto of "I serve an awesome God," rings loud and clear. Gene was the Good Shepherd who tended his flock and brought us to good pastures.

How is that I and everyone else Gene met, were all touched to the core, like we had known him all the days of our life? I think I met Gene's soul, cast in his beatific smile.

The easy side of God had shown Gene what lay ahead, that the seven days he could breathe would be his ultimate reward. And on the seventh day, God rested.

When I received the call that Gene had died, the weight of hurt was unbearable. Atlas could not carry it. A great mass of grief rose up in my throat at the unfairness of the world. Why? Why oh why? Malinda said this was just meant to be—the move, the weekend visits from family and friends, his new-found power to pray and best of all, the time she shared with Gene, one-on-one, for five months.

Melancholy rose up over me like a shroud. My throat was too tight to speak. The tears broke loose completely because I would never again hear his voice again, "The more you do on this side, the easier the other side will be." Never again see him smile or watch as he walked with his family. Never again see that twinkle in his eye.

The ravage of raw grief was such a painful shock to my system. Grief is taking all the space. It overtakes every part of me. I was not ready for the sheer physicality of it, the lead-lined overcoat of pain. Pain radiates from my body in waves. My chest hurt, my stomach pounded harder than my heart, my tears burned. Never see him pour gravy over his waffles, his pancakes, and his pulled-pork sandwich. For Gene, gravy was a condiment. Chocolate a dessert? Not for Gene.

If I could just get through pain to sorrow, I thought I could do sorrow. But I found grief is such a slippery slope, and many times trying to climb through the pain to sorrow, I fell backwards. Gene's death was a divorce no one asked for, and to live through it is to find a way to disengage from what I thought I could not stand to lose. Gene and I talked about how when this part of the journey was over he would buy a motor home and the four of us would vacation together. Never again see the four of us enjoying the fruits of the transplant. Never again see him fishing. Never. God I hate that word Never.

How do people survive? People die all the time, every hour, every day. Families all over the world staring at beds that are no longer slept in. Shoes that are no longer worn. Fishing poles sitting idly. Flannel jackets hanging on poles.

What do you remove? What do you clean? Trace after trace of Gene that will immutably erase. I want to put up stanchions and red velvet ropes in my mind, like they do in historical mansions. I tell Gene's story to get him back, to capture the traces of his footfalls in the snow. My past is the last link to Gene, and as much as it hurts, I wrap it around myself like a blanket.

I wonder does time heal, and if so, does it mean I have accepted the world without him? Time does not heal; time merely passes. Time does not heal as much as it buries things in the undergrowth of your brain, where things lie in wait to ambush you when you least expect it. I am not ready for time to heal this wound, but I also know I am powerless to stop its passing. I do not need for you to tell me this will happen. It is inevitable. The real hell of all this is I am going to get through it. Too many good people do not make it. Too many. The sadness sometimes drowns me, and I cannot get enough air. The names who have not made it pinball around my brain. The pain most times is no longer there, the slope a little less slippery, but the fond memories will sometimes bring me to tears.

Lung transplant is without a doubt a risk, but dying is a certainty. I know it's not all sunshine and lollypops. I know, pun intended, that life is not all gravy. I try to understand why such a good person as Gene is no longer alive, try to understand his death, but for me, it is like trying to decipher the theory of relativity. I try to make sense of his loss, and the too many others, but I cannot. There is no sense to it.

God only gives me what I can bear, but I cannot bear this. How did I live life with my lung disease? How did I survive? Why? Tell me why.

Yea, I walk through the valley of the shadow of death, not around it, or over it, or beside it. Through it. I know that the smallest of things in the valley, a smile, a couple, a southern twang, can send me back there. My grief is never smooth and there are pockets when all the memories and nostalgia surface.

Gene, you made the world a better place for Richard and me. I see your wife, Malinda, my good friend, who sits in the peaceful center of the eye of grief. Only by going through the most turbulent part of the storm can you find that place; and I see her delight in the memories, blowing out the sadness like a candle. I do worry, how slippery is her slope?

Gene taught me the time we have is a gift. Thanking me for my friendship—appreciating life's small things like his granddaughter's high school graduation. Know your limits and respect them, rely on others, need other people to help you out. He taught me that both Life and Death are two hard things to do alone.

Grief is the very heavy price I pay for love. It's a sadness that lodged itself in my throat like a pill that refuses to go down. A bitter pill to swallow. I know that sometimes I just have to soldier on in my own private, messy way. There is nothing like death to make you think about life.

Poet Robert Browning Hamilton rings true. "I walked a mile with Pleasure, she chattered all the way, but left me none the wiser, for all she had to say—I walked a mile with Sorrow, and ne'er a word said she, but, oh, the things I learned from her when Sorrow walked with me."

People told me that once this happened, or this passed, everything would be better. There is no timetable for grief and no expiration date for love. Some people told me you can only grieve for a year, like grief is a straight line, like a story book that has a beginning, middle and an end. There is no plot line to grief—one day I am fine, and the next back into a hole of grief for Gene, Monica, Karen C. and the father I see in my dreams with his arms crossed looking at the hospital bed of our Donor, and all the others who did not make it.

Gene had dignity, gentleness, gratefulness and a good nature for all he had been through. A true Southern gentleman. Deep devotion was reflected in his steadfast eyes, trust unwavering, loyalty unbounded, and his companionship a treasured gift. In his presence, we who were patients, caregivers and friends, were uplifted, inspired to do more and be more. I believe what Gene shared was a touch of heaven, a ministry of presence. I know now what peace looks like, and his smile will always burn in my heart.

I know to live on in the hearts of those we love is not to die. Everyone who loved you Gene, will love you still. Everyone whose lives you touched will continue to feel their lives, my life, diminished by your passing. Gene's legacy is his wife and children and grandchildren—this is his piece of the future and our piece of Gene.

God Bless you Gene. May the grace of God be with you Malinda. You have touched so many lives and made such a difference to so many.

I beg this day once more to push rewind, roll back this tide of history and travel back in time. Memories are the present he gave me, and I open them again and again. "You're not really going to eat that sausage slathered in gravy?" Death can never ever take away from me what I held. I am glad I remember. I know forgetting is worse than remembering.

I shall always remember Gene and the too many others who did not make it to the other side of transplant. I will never forget Gene, because if I do, I shall forget who I am. It was a privilege to love him.

I allow myself quiet moments until once again your face shines in my memory, and maybe this time, I will ladle gravy on my waffles. Chocolate anyone?

I know God has found a special place for Gene along a rolling stream with fish biting endlessly. I wonder how trout tastes with gravy. Gene, can you see me scrunching my nose? Can you hear me say Yuck?

The most meaningful thing I can say, I miss him too. *The most meaningful thing I can say, I miss him too.*

Saying good-bye is the hardest thing we're called upon to do in this world.

THERE ARE SOME BATTLES
THE OTHER SIDE

I stripped one of my friends of his stripes and reduced his rank to acquaintance, when he lobbed a grenade at my memories, saying Gene did not fight the good fight—he did not battle, for he only lived 7 days. I hear Malinda's voice, that Gene relished every breath he took for those seven days. His granddaughter, Hailey, had asked her grandmother why the other people she met who had had a transplant had not died. Malinda honestly answered, that Poppa must have been sicker than we thought and how happy I was that those other people were enjoying God's gift because I know how happy Gene was for seven wonderful days.

Did Gene die from COPD because he did not fight the disease hard enough? Did he die because he did not fight the good fight? No, no, no—a thousand nos. Of course not. I hear the well-intentioned but misguided words and phrases that have become ingrained in the lung disease lexicon. Lost a battle with; gave the fight everything he had, fought the good fight, never backed down from a fight, a warrior to the end. Common clichés. We have heard them all.

This was no fight for Gene. This man was faced with a rotten hand of cards. What matters is he gave meaning to his life, and to so many others. In the end Gene lost his battle to COPD, his heart, and the unknown. COPD never really wins. It thinks it does, but it died also.

Equating the disease to a war against the enemy, fighting an adversary, or suffering in order to survive diminishes our understanding of the challenges, and the complexities faced by Gene, other patients and their families. Each person is different. Every disease is different. Each person comes to transplant differently.

The idea that Gene was waging a battle which he lost demeans him. Gene did not lose to an adversary. Emphasizing a lung patient's bravery and courage; that you are a warrior implies that if you can not conquer your disease, there is something wrong with you as a person, some weakness or flaw. If your lung disease progresses rapidly or you do not live to see the 8th day after transplant, it is your fault. Your willpower failed.

No one had a better attitude towards living. To say that Gene lost his fight implies that he had a say over his life. Gene did not choose any of that any more than I could have chosen the color of my eyes or hair. It is that arbitrary.

You have a choice, like Karyn or Gene, to play the cards dealt to you up or down, good or bad. This is what Karyn and Gene did. This is so much more empowering than the idea you can somehow control the ultimate outcome if you just fight hard enough.

You can bring yourself down and it can be the worst of the worst or you can be like Gene or Karyn and can carry on. I will deal with this on a daily basis. Know this my former friend without stripes, in this world there are simply wars that cannot be won, no matter how valiantly they are fought.

PERCHANCE TO DREAM
NO SIDES

It is the year 2042, and my son's yet-to-be born daughter is now 30, and she is at her new doctor's office, answering intake questions.

Do you have any allergies?

Does anyone in the family have any history of blood pressure?

Does anyone in the family have any history of liver disease?

Does anyone in the family have any history of lung disease?

"Yes, my Grandma Karyn had LAM."

The doctor pauses, looks up, and responds, "I have never met any woman who had LAM. I have only read about LAM."

After all, it was cured back in the 20's."

To dream.

MY BIRTHDAY
THE OTHER SIDE

Dear Donor,

I am remembering sadness. It makes me sad, not for now, but for what Karyn had been through. The stony weight of memories bear down on me. There are moments when I wish I could roll back the clock and take all the sadness away, but I know if I could, the joy would be gone as well. Someone told me recently that Karyn had been to hell and back and once I might have agreed but this journey on the bend in the road taken, so reluctantly, opened our eyes to scenery, the beauty of which we might otherwise have missed. It was a journey I would never replace with anything else. It taught me to love beyond myself, beyond anything and just love. It was beautiful and painful and precious and tender and generous and . . . it was our life and I am so lucky to say with tears welling, it is our life. I am living the life I want to live because I am living it with Karyn.

The past is always your past, yours. Even when you try to forget it, the past remembers you. I am glad that when we married almost forty years ago my life did not come with previews; otherwise, I might have thought it was too frightening to stay for the feature presentation and missed some really good parts. When I bought, I bought as-is, with no returns. All sales are final.

Karyn has been quite a read. Sometimes I had to fight to stay awake turning to the last pages of the book to find out how it ends. A book with suspense, unexpected turns, hope, and despair and heroic actions, a beautiful damsel in distress and snatches from the jaws of hell. Why couldn't life be more routine than plot?

It's a Once Upon a Time tale, framed within the magical thinking of a children's tale, where the forests of DUKE are enchanted and the lung monsters vincible, where love and courage always trump danger.

A wealth of emotions bubbling out and over. Donor, as you know, Karyn was snatched back from the foggy line where life rubs shoulders with death. A life lost, a life given back and my heart overflows. You can feel the good air in and around her.

The beauty of Karyn's message is that it is eternal. Karyn had hope in the beginning of her LAM struggle, and has it today. LAM exploded in her body, but it never ever touched her heart, and that's where hope lives. I search my heart for some warm memories. Who says reruns are awful? I close my eyes and it is her I see. I think of love and it is her.

Donor, there is an unbreakable bond between us,

Karyn, I love you; three very tiny words, they take up so brief a space, but they fill up all the space in my heart,

All my love,

Richard

Dear Donor,

You are etched upon my heart forever.

I have outlived my original expiration date, and each day is a gift to me that I seize. I walk my dog and not my second dog tank. This journey has been incredible. A reminder of how precious life is every day. If it was taken from me tomorrow, I would be okay because I have learned to forgive easily, to appreciate the sunrise and sunset, and to love with my whole heart.

My steps are blended into Richard's as we walk, our hands come easily together. The sky is clear and blue, and I see us talking, laughing, planning dinner, deciding what movie to see—I mean these are not life shattering moments I am talking about! They are just good days when we share our lives. I am struck by the simple truth that sometimes the most ordinary things can be made extraordinary simply by doing them with the right person. I inhale the moment often, every day.

While every moment of my life is a "dream come true," as my granddaughter says, I do have fears. Fears that I will have a rejection (don't take it personally) that can't be treated, fear of getting sick, or maybe my LAM will come back, but I try to put all that in the back of my mind. I try not to worry about life too much because I have read the last page of the Book and it turns out all right. I suppose we would all prefer our fairy tales to be simple, but they're not. The future will reveal itself when it's time. I can wait.

We have to live our lives as best we can in the present, and living and loving as much as we can every day with no regrets. LAM, COPD, CF, automobile accidents, heart attacks. That darn bus. We just never know. Time has a way of zipping by, the mile markers racking up so fast, whole decades disappear from sight in the rearview mirror. Whoosh!

Maybe some can afford to wait, maybe for them, there's a tomorrow. Maybe for them, there's one thousand tomorrows, or five thousand, or ten thousand. So much time they can bathe in it, roll around in it, let it slide like pennies through their fingers. So much time, they can waste it, but for some of us, there is only today and the truth is, you never know. As you and I know, Donor, every moment you have is precious.

My air flows in and out of your lungs, taking sustenance into my body, and delivering my leftovers back to the world. The flow of my breath, from my first cry to my last exhale, is my basic function, connecting my heart and brain to life. You and I have become each other's air. I can taste it.

You and I Donor are destined to share our souls now and forever.

If anyone asks about Richard and me, just tell them we are out on a long walk, with our dog, breathing in the sky and sunlight.

Sometimes life may be hard, but it comes as natural as breathing.

With all my breath,

Karyn

Dear Donor,

Five years ago today, I adopted Willie and Jake from Colorado Sheltie rescue, they became my two Delta Pet Partner therapy dogs. I had lost my forever dog, Tyler, suddenly, and wanted an older dog to replace Ty Boy. Little Willie was 11 ½ when we adopted him, and he lived a few months past his 14 ½ year marker.

It was my birthday, as it is today, and I whined and whined and begged and begged that it would be my best birthday present ever, if I could have both dogs. What I should have said to Karyn was that getting both dogs would be a very good present, but not my best, "Getting both dogs would be a very good present, but it cannot compare to all the other parties and gifts you have given me on my birthday in the past." But I stuck to the "best" line. "This would be my best-ever birthday gift, if I could have both of them." After an hour of intense whining, Karyn caved and Willie and his two year old "brother," Jake, came into our household.

Last night, as we were walking six miles, Karyn apologized to me that she had not bought me a birthday present. Yes she had. For my birthday this year, I got my wife back.

Karyn is making up for lost past time, and future times that may be lost. Misplaced time. Found time. For as you can see, Donor, I am having an affair with my wife.

This year, the best birthday present ever. Ever. "Richard, blow out the candles. Make a wish."

I already did.

Karyn's body may be pretty dinged up, but the inside is more beautiful than ever. You know what I love about you Karyn? *"What?"* And I answered "everything." Karyn, keep breathing, just keep doing it, in and out, in and out. After all these years, you take my breath away. I am having an affair with my wife.

I have been asked many times, would we go through this again? If we had known all the problems? In a breath. I suppose we would all prefer our fairy tales to be simple, but they're not.

The three of us lungketeers have become each other's air. I can taste the sweetness. Memories have been hermetically sealed and perfectly preserved. It seems like yesterday; it seems like eternity. Sometimes remembering all that has happened is hard, but I remember it all because I remember it all. And somehow that comes as natural as breathing.

I will always have one thing no matter what, one thing that time will never take from me, the story that happened here. The Story of Us.

Donor, sometimes you think you are at the end of the book, but it's only the end of a chapter.

One for all,

Richard

MAY 2010

THE OTHER SIDE

Good Friends Fill the Heart—an Ode to our Special Caregivers

Twice during the six months at DUKE, I returned home to our children, grandchild, work and chores. Without the help of our alternate caregivers, I could not have balanced life. I was home briefly when my sister Pam called that Karyn had received the Gift of Life. I returned home for three weeks a month out, and Karyn's good friends, Helene, who handed the baton to Randee, came after to Durham.

To be a caregiver rightly requires a large gift of patience, grace and peace. It can be a wearying job, a full time job with little time for oneself. There is always supper to get or breakfast to be fetched, lunch to be made. There are dishes to be washed, clothes to be washed. Grocery lists to be made, groceries to be bought. Laying out the clothes and voila, you have become a valet. Above all, to differentiate what is important and what is not important.

Trust me on this one, your loved one's fears, anxieties and sense of dignity will correlate directly with your own. The biggest challenge of a caregiver is in your own attitudes, and our three caregivers staying with Karyn helped my wife dip her toes back into life, a little bit at a time.

Our caregivers are my heroes. Just ordinary people who are confronted with an overwhelming situation, but rise above and do more than you would ever think possible with little regard for themselves. Just trying to be there and help Karyn is the focus.

Helene related to me, "It's something we don't even think about, we just do. We move forward, we find a way to cope, and we do it all in honor of the person we love."

My sister said late one night, "To not give is like wrapping a present and not giving it. You just try to give away what you want yourself. It's the only thing that makes you what you are."

At the one year anniversary, to honor our caregivers, Karyn brought all three to San Antonio to celebrate her Gift. At work, I celebrated by giving my two employees a bonus. How the two of them kept the ship afloat amazes me on the many days the phone never stops ringing.

Each of our caregivers is different, each one with different gifts. Each one offers Karyn something uniquely their own. One listens, one offers advice, one makes you laugh, and one takes you shopping. They're always near, a gentle touch, a helping hand. It's good to be in safe hands. Each one of their gifts is a cherished treasure of a beautiful friendship, never judging Karyn, just loving her. How good it is to be loved. The caregiver's presence; that you are simply there lets Karyn know that she is loved, respected, and not alone.

Yes, they did find time to shop and buy stuff. But I'm here to tell you, better than any iPad or sweater, was their gift in Durham, of these special caregiver friends, including Lammie Susie, and their special presence.

Too many people just passing by are led to buy things and fill their lives with stuff. But friends, true friends, don't come with price tags and that is why they are truly wonderful gifts.

Our three caregivers and Carolina Susie left footprints in my heart. A shared laugh, a tear, and a hug. You never said no, or you can't. If you need me, I'll be there for you. To know that someone cares, a kindness spread like sunshine. You chose to make a difference and lifted our burden and lightened our load. You knew what was important. I am so very grateful.

I remember Helene's words, "We can do just about anything to help our loved one get through. We know our days will change, our routines will be rewritten (Is there time to write all that needs to be done?)." Randee exclaimed, "But we do whatever it takes, because we would do anything, anything at all. We're caregivers!"

I am sure you're familiar with the old saying, "You can't take it with you." They must have been talking about the blouses and the flat screens, because good friends, good caregivers, being there, fill the heart. And you can take that with you, anywhere you go. As Karyn said, "Friends are like good bras. They are supportive, hard to find, and close to the heart."

I hope all of you had a great time in San Antonio, and as Dr. Seuss said best, "Don't cry because it is over. Smile because it happened."

Our life is given to us, and we earn it by giving it. To be able to touch someone's life and to know in your heart of hearts that giving is true having.

You caregivers are my forever heroes.

Once a caregiver . . . .

Love,

Richard

ROLLER COASTER
BOTH SIDES NOW

I feel like I am on a roller coaster. LAM and Lung Transplant have been like a roller coaster ride, one which has required every ounce of my willpower to stay on. Yes, having a double lung transplant and LAM is like being trapped on a roller coaster, a really good one with lots of twists and turns and huge drops. You know the kind that make your stomach turn over. Every once in a while, someone changes the ride: new drops, new twists, new fears. Don't they have roller coasters that only go up?

LAM in a way changed my calendar. We go by days. We take them one day at a time. I've gotten used to the roller coaster, at least as much as I can. It sure would be nice to get a nice level stretch for a while and let Richard and me catch our breath, settle our stomachs, and get ready for that next drop. But this isn't that kind of ride, I guess. No slow spots, no timeouts. It's full speed every day.

Waiting for the check-ups of my FEV1 and the other tests at Duke and knowing, really knowing, that all is well. Those monthly blood draws to monitor my medications, and the waiting for results. The wait. That's my ride. The ticket was bought, you take the ride. Couldn't there have been a height requirement?

Having acute rejection from aspergillis, from someone just mowing their lawn, getting a little sick and having pneumonia and being in the hospital, desaturating and watching my O2 drop into the low 80's, watching my kidney scores go from bad to worse. Those are the little drops that make my stomach turn over.

As much as the twists and turns of the ride affect me physically, the ups and downs also play havoc with my emotions. I look for hope where I find it. I yearn to return to Duke to learn there is no rejection and a clear bronch. I brace myself for bad news, and when it comes, acute rejection, aspergillis, it still hits harder than I was prepared for. I smile and reassure everyone around me that the ride isn't too bad. Other times I can only admit that the last drop really got to me.

After a while, I forget what it was like to not be on the ride. That life on solid ground is over, at least for now. My ticket is for a truly wild ride, and there's really no way to get off. And no one else, not even my husband, as much as he wants to, as much as he needs to; no one else can really ride along with me. Rich can watch. Rich can be supportive but when I am up there on top of the ride, looking down on that huge drop in front of me, I am the only one in the car.

Keep your hands up Karyn, and scream real loud. It's really hard to catch your breath when you desaturate. Hold on tight, both to your seat, and to me. You're about ten feet tall in my eyes. I wish that at the bottom of the hill, you'd get a giant wave of cold water in your face, and a hidden camera would snap your picture while some hairy character dances around, or maybe I've been to Disneyland too many times.

But you are learning to throw your arms up in the air and scream like crazy. In fact, yell wheeeeeee, and you will feel better, and if you have faith that the car won't jump the tracks, the view from the top can be truly amazing.

I know that sometimes your stomach drops as if you'd just crested the tallest peak on the roller coaster and you are about to barrel down the other side, careening down at frightening speed. So all you can do is hold your hands up in the air, and yell as you ride down this transplant hill, knowing that on the other side, there will be a long climb upward to the top of the next hill. We just have to keep up with it. Actually, I'd better stay one step ahead.

A roller coaster, a ride that can make you frightened, scared, sick, excited and so thrilled altogether. Often I feel like I am in line, knowing that the ride is scary but that you will walk off the ramp when it's all over, when we no longer count the days or years post-. I know you will walk off, shaky legs perhaps, but still walking, with big smiles on your face and the faces of those of us who have watched, cheered and loved you.

It hits me on the head, and I realize how much those of us living without LAM, or a double lung transplant, or a lung disease, take for granted our life on the ground.

Hold fast and thanks for sharing your strength.

I love you,

Richard

A HEARSE NEVER COMES WITH LUGGAGE RACKS
BOTH SIDES

Dear Donor,

Did LAM or the lung transplant make me a better person? I do not think so, just a different person. I know some things now that I wouldn't have known otherwise, but who's to say I wouldn't have learned different things in that other life?

My LAM surely has humbled me. My LAM surely gave me love of life. That does not mean that LAM is not what it is, hard and difficult, but we all have the opportunity to make what we can of what we are given. LAM on its own did not do this for me. LAM and transplant were merely the catalyst for it, and I snatched the opportunity.

As a LAMMIE and a post-transplant, I am living and dying at the same time. If LAM comes back, it comes back. If there is chronic rejection, there is not a lot I can do about it. My life is in flux, unique to me, and shared by others. The living seems so intense, filled with exquisite beauty and wonder, the dying feels like tearing away all the layers, seeing parts of me I did not know were there, and it hurts, but just a little.

Knowing that there may be little time left, LAM and transplant caused me to speak more directly and honestly, since there is no time to beat around the bush. How a potential expiration date was liberating.

I truly think of others and pray for them. I have such empathy that it hurts sometimes. I have learned that everyone suffers no more than the other. I never assume that my pain is greater merely because it is mine. My own adversity has enabled me to see clearly that I only have to look around to see the struggles of others, now through a different prism. I can now fully appreciate their struggle and the nobility that they demonstrate in the face of overwhelming adversity. I feel a sort of aching toward my fellow humans, all of us just stumbling along, doing the best we can.

I am also learning to stretch my forgiveness muscles. I am learning gentleness and a lightness of being. To live large and travel light, trusting in the power of kindness and love to lead me where I need to go. My LAM and transplant taught me that getting old is worth fighting for, and that social status is not really important. I have learned there are a lot of people who really do care and are very kind, and my LAM and transplant truly brought out the very best in people.

My LAM and transplant gave me love of life. I love more deeply and I give more readily. I love waking up every morning to be here, alive. I can remember the past and plan for the future, but I can only truly live right now. I do not look over my shoulder or try to see my future living for some other time. I live for the now. To love harder and deeper, and appreciate the absolute beauty in every day and its blessings because right now is all I've got. My happiness is deeper, my sadness is more profound, and my tolerance for the trivial is gone. I now see the sky bluer than ever before. The rain does not bother me. I see shapes in the clouds like when I was a kid. I am reborn.

Donor, before LAM and transplant, life just seemed to happen. Now life seems more . . . . more what? More acknowledged, more deliberate, more intense? Maybe just more. I feel more everything. Now I think of life as a terminal illness, so I love it with a joy and a passion as it ought to be lived. I remember that everything changed that day, the day I figured out there was exactly enough time for all the important things in life.

I am aware of life and how precious and beautiful it is. LAM and transplant made me aware just how short life is, and that every moment should be lived to its fullest and that nothing, nothing is more satisfying than love given and received. Life and love are now, this minute, today. Tomorrow will take care of itself.

Knowledge and wisdom did not come to me like a robe and a crown that I put on and suddenly had all the answers. There is no curtain to look behind for the answers. Rather, wisdom and knowledge have come from living through these raw experiences over time.

I have learned it is okay to be sad and feel those huge feelings. I have learned that when I am hurting, I do not have to do it alone. I can cry on the shoulder of my husband or a close friend. I have learned that life is fragile, and not to be taken for granted. I have learned to accomplish tasks I would rather not do at all. I have learned to be brave in the face of difficulties. I have learned to laugh at life, rather than life laughing at me. I have learned that not one day I spend on earth has been promised to me; this is simply the price I pay for that first breath I took in the beginning. I have heard the siren call of mortality and I understand what is now will never be again.

I learned not to worry about things I cannot control. I believe things take their own course, happen for a reason. I was not always that way. I used to think I could control everything. I am much happier for having stopped trying. I have no control over much of what happens to me in my life but I do have control over how to react to it. Looking for the answer to Why Me is futile. But there are answers to the What Now. Once I took responsibility for my reactions, I was free to live again. Making the best of my experience, the wake of dawn, and giving it meaning, that's my choice. This was not an easy lesson.

Stay in the moment. I am not afraid to die. I just do not want to. I love life that you gave me, and living.

I would trade these "gains" for a longer life without LAM and transplant, but they are pretty good consolation prizes. I have learned so much and lived so much. You can be told about LAM, about lung disease, about lung transplant, but unless you live it, it won't mean much. I was here and I lived through this. And this is what I learned. You just can't put an old head on young shoulders. I guess what I am really talking about is some way to tell those who follow in my footsteps, "You are not alone."

No matter what, I spend the time breathing and living and not counting the time until I am not. And maybe that's one of the lessons here. In spite of the LAM, the lung transplant, the rejection drugs, in spite of what those of us have been through, we're all just human.

The scars may be healed but my gift of life is on a clock that is ticking. You, my gift's original owner, have already gone on ahead of me, and it is only time before I too will be reunited with you, my donor. I do not live in shadows of that fear. I choose to live my life looking forward to each day and to the future. The gratitude I feel to you is indescribable. A sigh of relief comes from deep within me, and one deep breath says it all.

Life is exhilarating and breath-taking and beautiful. Donor, I know that whatever happens I can get through this. I never let LAM, nor the anti-rejection drugs steal the goodness from my days. Maybe life is not fair; it's just fairer than death, that's all.

I am like everyone else, except that I'm not. I am enjoying the life you gave to me a breath at a time. Life is after all, a breath.

The things I bought for my children may last a few months or a few years, but what I have taught them and others through my adversity, what I showed all, will last their lifetimes. It is so true that you can't take it with you, which is why there are no luggage racks on a hearse, and for me, I shall have no luggage.

You are not alone,

Karyn

A LIFE LOST, A LIFE GIVEN BACK
BOTH SIDES

Dear Donor,

My life was becoming smaller and smaller. I was hibernating. No one wants to live through another person's death, but it is part of the deal. Isn't it sick hoping for someone to die? I live because you died. For me to live, someone's family had to grieve so I may be happy. It is a rough equation but the only way I can live. A life lost, a life given back, and my heart overflows.

To know that when you died, your family cared enough to give a complete stranger the gift of life, the family who at the worst moment in their life, generously chose to save my world. I am so grateful and I cannot even begin to express how I feel with words. To know that my good fortune was borne out of the depths of such sadness is about as conflicted as I can feel.

Organ donation is truly a miracle. I felt like someone had been sitting on my chest for ten years and finally had decided to get off. To be restored surpasses any gift than can be given. I have been given a gift that is tangible and livable. A gift that I live minute by minute, hour by hour, day in and day out. These minutes, hours, days, would not be possible without your gift. God Bless You.

You are right here with me. I wish I could feel your lungs, touch your lungs, and could touch you. One thing is very certain; because of you, each day is sunnier than the previous day. Tomorrow has endless possibilities, and that is nothing short of a miracle.

I do what I can because I can, and to do anything less than the best I can do is to sacrifice the gift of life and my second chance. I do know that I live to honor you, the person who saved my life. I am the caretaker, and your lungs are like my child I must protect.

Know that I am forever connected to you. You are etched upon my heart forever. We are destined to share our souls, now and forever. I, who made it to the other side, live as a memorial to you. More than just lungs, you gave me life. You did not just give me back my life, you gave back all of the lives of all the people in my life.

I hope and pray that one day soon your family will respond to my letters and get in touch with me so I can thank them in person for giving me this beautiful new life, for the use of your loaner, to know in this very unique way, their child is still living in this world.

For me to see firsthand how precious life is and then get another day to live, to appreciate the gift of deep breaths, I shall never forget that I could not breathe at all. I live my life to the fullest and every moment is full of wonder. You gave me back myself.

I have been given a great gift, the knowledge of my own mortality.

The first breath I take when I wake up each morning reminds me to be thankful.

You renewed my life, and we have become each other's air.

Everything. Wordless and spoken. Everything. Written and understood.

All of me,

Karyn

Dear Donor,

How do I say thank you to you, that my wife is alive today because of your gift of her life saving lungs? How do I really say thank you that my wife is alive? I want you to know that my wife, Karyn, cried when she was told the operation was a go, that she would receive your lungs. She cried because she knew that somewhere a family lost a precious beloved person in their life.

My heart goes out to you and to your family and my heart will always be there. I am overwhelmed with feelings, a most curious mix of joy and sorrow.

Our Bible says in Ruth, that "She who saves a single life saves the entire world." When I think of all the people who love the woman you saved, who rely on Karyn, whose lives would be so fundamentally different without her, you not only saved someone's life for sure, but even more important, you saved Karyn's world. You gave my wife her life back, and you gave to all the lives of all the people in her life.

I love you because you saved my wife's life. Karyn was the one dying, but in a way, I felt my soul slipping away.

Now Karyn gets to grow older. She will see her grandchildren grow up. She will walk her dogs. She will breathe. She will dance again. She will climb mountains again. She will be.

Remember that no matter where I am or what I am doing, I have a special place inside me for you. It's been there since the day we met and you breathed life into my wife and partner. Your place in my heart is tender, a bruise of longing, a pulse of unfinished business.

Just remembering May 17th pushes and pulls at me in a thousand, million ways. My memories circle and circle, random, out of order, and not always complete. There is always one that comes back again and again: Karyn reaching out to me, grasping my shoulders and arm, walking in the hallways at Duke, her fingers entwined in my fingers, which I take and do not let go.

Your lungs breathing life into my wife and me.

Know that forever I shall hold you in my heart, my soul, my tears and my every breath.

Maybe all I should say is that reliable old line that goes on almost every postcard, "Having a great time, wish you were here."

May God bring peace to you and your family,

Richard

Sadly, our letters to the donor's family go unanswered. I need closure to meet your family, to have your family touch Karyn's chest and see her breathe through your lungs. We may never have met, but you always will be part of my wife and me. Grafting your lungs into my wife, taking something from one person, attaching it to another person, until they grow together. We have become each other's air. I can taste it.

I do not know if this scene is true or not as all information about the donor is confidential, and God I am hopeful that in the near future we will meet your family and I will find out. I see this scene over and over again; an endless spool of film. I see your father standing sentinel by your hospital bed. His back is to me and I do not see you, his daughter, or his wife. I know your age is 15. The father takes a deep sigh, and crosses his arms. I see your father look down at his shoes, looks at the hospital bed. He steps back and crosses his arms, as if he is guarding himself against any more pain or maybe as though holding his loved one, one more time in his arms. His arms wrapped across his chest, hands hugging his shoulders. His voice not breaking, voice already broken. I can see his back contracting and expanding as he breathes deeply. His head is nodding, saying yes to what his heart cannot yet accept.

A vent tube is taped to your face, and a machine hisses softly, doing the job his daughter could no longer do on her own. A voice murmurs, "Tell her good-bye." His face is blinded by tears. Your dying, the dying of his daughter, fills his world. You will always be 15. You will not learn to drive and he will not cover his eyes while you almost hit the car in front of you. He will not beam with pride as your date whisks you away in your specially-picked-out beautiful prom dress. He will not walk you down the aisle, and give you away. He will not caress your baby. You will always be 15.

It's the last day, the last few hours, then moments, and then moment. He reaches out to touch you, one last time, while your body is still warm and before the ventilator, keeping you breathing and alive, is unplugged. His body is wracked by tears. He has trouble standing, his knees almost crumbling. The dying of his daughter fills his universe. The last time he will say good-bye. The last time he will hug you.

Blessedly, your memories with him are the presents you gave him, and he will open them again and again. Tears roll down his face and my face.

There is no age limit on who can donate deceased organs. There are no age limits for living donation and tissue donation; the deciding factor on whether a person can donate is the person's physical condition, not age. Most major religions support donation and have provided statements for their membership.

Every effort is made to save the patient's life before donation can be considered. Donor families are not charged for the medical costs associated with organ donation and tissue retrieval. Donation surgery includes careful reconstruction of the body and should not interfere with funeral plans, including open casket services.

More than 119,000 people are waiting right now for organs. Sadly, eighteen people each day die waiting for an organ. Every 11 minutes, a new person needing an organ is added to the list. Become a donor. Be the One for someone's special Karyn.

In life starting out, we all want to be the one to make a difference; we all think we will make a difference, but the truth of the matter is very few of us will ever make that difference. But like our donor, the last thing you do in life can make that difference.

Be the Difference.

DonateLifeAmerica.Org.

GLOSSARY OF TERMS

Acute rejection—Early immune rejection to transplanted lungs where the immune system detects the new lungs as foreign and tries to mount an inflammatory response against them. Acute rejection occurs in approximately 60 per cent of patients in the first year after transplantation and is diagnosed by biopsy during bronchoscopy. Acute rejection is treated with steroids and other medications that suppress the immune system

Angiomyolipoma (AML)—a benign tumor (oma) consisting of blood vessels (angio), muscles (myo), and fat (lipo). AMLS occur in LAM and are most often found in the kidneys

Arterial Blood gas (ABG)—A measurement of the oxygen and carbon dioxide in the blood obtained by drawing a blood sample from an artery (usually the radial artery near one's wrist or in the brachial artery in the crook of the arm) rather than a vein. The ABG measures the amount of oxygen that your blood is able to carry to your body tissues. The ABG measures acidity (pH) and the level of oxygen and carbon dioxide in the blood. The pH of blood is usually between 7.35 and 7.45. A pH of less than 7.0 is called acid and a pH greater than 7.0 is called basic (alkaline). Blood is slightly basic, and Bicarbonate ($HC03$) is a chemical buffer that keeps the pH of blood from becoming too acidic or too basic.

Bilateral lung transplant—Receiving two lungs during a transplant. Also called a double-lung transplant.

Biopsy—A small sample of tissue taken from an organ for diagnostic purposes

BIPAP, CPAP, DPAP—P.A.P. stands for positive airway pressure. These assist in the physical needs for breathing, but also help remove excess $CO2$

from the system. BiPAP stands for Bilevel Positive Airway pressure and the BiPAP provides 2 sets of pressure to assist in inspiration (breathing in) and exhalation (breathing out). The pressures keep the airway from collapsing on the lungs.

Bleb—A cyst full of fluid and/or air on or near the surface of the lungs.

Bronchiolitis obliterans syndrome (BOS)—Small airway scarring. There are no proven treatments for BOS, which causes a significant limiting factor to long term survival after lung transplantation. Five years after transplant 50% of lung transplant patients have died from BOS.

Bronchoscopy—A procedure where physicians look into the lungs and surrounding airways using a small camera, a thin flexible fiber optic tube. The tube is passed through the nose or mouth or trach down into the airways (bronchi) checking for infection and rejection.

Buspar—Treats certain anxiety disorders, or to relieve the symptoms of anxiety and/or depression

Cardiac Catherization—Procedure in a which a small tube is guided through a vein or artery into the right side or left side of the heart, to check function of heart and coronary arteries

Chest tubes—Sterile tubes inserted into the chest cavity between the lung and chest wall; used to re-inflate the lung, to release air, or to drain chyle or another fluid from the area.

Chronic Obstructive Pulmonary Disease—COPD—An obstructive lung disease most frequently caused by smoking. Although LAM is also an obstructive lung disease, most physicians do not refer to it as COPD.

Chronic rejection—scar tissue in the small airways of the lungs. There is no effective treatment for this condition.

Citracal—A calcium supplement, which is used by persons, who are unable to get enough calcium in their regular diet or who have a need for additional calcium. Citracal is used to prevent or treat several conditions that may cause hypocalcemia (not enough calcium in the blood). The body requires calcium to make strong bones. Calcium is also needed for the heart, muscles, and nervous system to work properly.

Collapsed Lung—A condition where the space between the chest wall and lung is filled with air or fluid causing the lung to deflate partially or completely. Also called a pneumo or pneumothorax.

Cyclosporine—Immunosuppressant drug medication used to prevent transplant rejection, which works by decreasing the activity of the immune system, counteracting white blood cells rejecting the transplanted lungs

Diabetes—Body's inability to control the amount of insulin or blood sugar it produces for energy

FEV1—The percent of the vital capacity that can be forcibly expelled in the first second of maximal expiration. The maximum amount of air you can forcibly exhale in the lungs, and used to determine the severity of obstruction and/or restriction in the airways. FEV1 is a marker for degree of obstruction, greater than 80% of predicted is normal. Less than 40% is considered severe obstruction.

Gastroesophageal reflux disease (GERD)—Stomach contents leak backwards from the stomach into the esophagus. Evaluated before and after transplant by impedance testing, with a 24 hour pH testing, esophageal manometry, barium swallow or stomach emptying studies.

Gastrostomy—Jejunostomy The GJ tube is a tube placed into the stomach and small intestine. The tube vents the stomach for air or drainage and alternate way to feed

Immunosuppression—Preventing the body's immune system from rejecting an organ transplant

Imuran—Prevents rejection of a transplanted lung, and is an immunosuppressive agent

Nissen Fundiplication—Stomach wrap done by surgery to treat gastroeophageal reflux disease. The top part of the stomach is sewn 360 degrees around the esophagus to prevent stomach contents from re-entering the esophagus

Nystatin—Antifungal mouthwash agent used to prevent infections, such as Thrush

O2—Oxygen—Auxiliary oxygen use usually expressed as number of liters per minutes/hours per day/days per week—for example, 2L, 24/7—Supplemental oxygen provides oxygen as concentrations greater than room air to raise oxygen levels in the blood. Oxygen delivery systems can be stationary, such as home concentrator, or portable, such as liquid and canister systems. Oxygen can be received through nasal cannula or mask.

PFT—Pulmonary Function Test—(PFT's)—tests that measure the volume of air that is inhaled and exhaled. PFT's also measure gases, such as oxygen and carbon dioxide in the lungs

Pneumothorax—A lung collapse—"Pneumo" refers to air and "thorax" to the chest cavity. In LAM, a pneumothorax occurs when one of the cysts (blebs) bursts and air leaks into the space around the lungs. The pressure of air between the lung and the chest wall forces the lung to collapse. Sudden shortness of breath, a dry cough, cyanosis (turning blue) and sharp pain felt in the chest, back, and/or arms are the main symptoms.

Prednisone—Mimics the effects of hormones body produces naturally in adrenal glands. A Corticosteroid, which also suppresses the immune system, and can help control conditions in which body's immune system mistakenly attacks its own tissues

Prograf—Immunosuppressant, similar to Cyclosporine

Protonix—Treats certain conditions in which there is too much acid in the stomach. Treats erosive esophagitis or "heartburn" caused by GERD, a condition where the acid in the stomach washes back up into the esophagus.

Pulse Oximeter—(Pulse Ox)—painless test in which a sensor is placed on the finger or earlobe to measure the level of oxygen saturation in the blood. Does not determine if carbon dioxide is being removed from the system.

Rejection—immune response that occurs when a transplanted lung is not the organ in the body at birth. Immune system sees the organ as a foreign invader and acts against it. If left untreated rejection can result in organ failure.

Septra—a sulfa drug used to treat infection such as serious forms of pneumonia

Spirometry test—A series of breathing tests that provides information about the extent of lung disease and how well the lungs function. The test measures how much (volume) and how fast (flow) you can move air into and out of your lungs

Thrush—Yeast infection of the mucus membrane lining the mouth and tongue, caused by forms of fungus called Candida. Persons who have diabetes and high blood sugar levels are more likely to get oral thrush because the extra sugar in saliva acts like food for Candida.

Tracheostomy—Surgically made hole that goes through the front of the neck and into the trachea. A breathing tube, also called a trach tube is put through the tracheostomy and directly into the windpipe to help the patient breathe

UNOS—United Network for Organ Sharing—National Agency that maintains a national computerized transplant waiting list, and helps locate donor organs. Scores are listed from 0 to 100. 1 being no need, and 100 almost dead.

Valcyte—Treats cytomegalovirus (CMV), a herpes-type virus. Every person is either CMV positive or CMV negative. Most of the population is positive, meaning they have been exposed to the virus and have developed antibodies for it. People who are negative have no antibodies for this virus. CMV infects the salivary glands, Symptoms, if any, resemble mononucleosis. CMV can cause serious illness if a person is immunosuppressed (for example, after a transplant).

Ventilator—A machine that helps a patient breathe, controls and monitors flow of air to the lungs. After surgery, a ventilator is used to help the new lungs expand completely.

Made in the USA
San Bernardino, CA
18 July 2014